Colonel Frédéric

The Description of Corsica

with an account of its union to the crown of Great Britain. Including the life of

General Paoli, and the memorial peresented to the National Assembly of France,

upon the forests in that island

Colonel Frédéric

The Description of Corsica
with an account of its union to the crown of Great Britain. Including the life of General Paoli, and the memorial peresented to the National Assembly of France, upon the forests in that island

ISBN/EAN: 9783337268152

Printed in Europe, USA, Canada, Australia, Japan

Cover: Foto ©Andreas Hilbeck / pixelio.de

More available books at **www.hansebooks.com**

THE

DESCRIPTION

OF

CORSICA,

WITH AN

ACCOUNT OF ITS UNION

TO THE

CROWN OF GREAT BRITAIN,

INCLUDING THE

LIFE OF GENERAL PAOLI,

AND

THE MEMORIAL

PRESENTED TO THE

NATIONAL ASSEMBLY OF FRANCE,

UPON THE

FORESTS IN THAT ISLAND,

WITH

A PLAN HIGHLY BENEFICIAL TO BOTH STATES,

ILLUSTRATED, WITH A MAP OF CORSICA.

DEDICATED TO HIS MAJESTY,

———————

BY *FREDERICK,*

SON OF THE LATE THEODORE, KING OF CORSICA.

———————

LONDON:

PRINTED FOR G. G. AND J. ROBINSON, PATER-NOSTER-ROW.

1795.

To the KING.

PERMIT me to lay before your Majesty the Description of Corsica, a Kingdom to which the late King Theodore had the best of rights by the unsolicited invitation, and voluntary submission of the People, his salutary laws, and the manner, truly paternal, he governed them. But his virtues found a strong adversary in the times. Several Sovereigns leagued against him, and a disgraceful dungeon, in this very Metropolis, was his reward.

May

May your Majesty's reign over the Corsicans be permanent, and peaceable, and may the British Flag ride for ever triumphant in those Seas by this new acquisition. These were the views of that sacrificed Monarch. These are the wishes of him, who is, with the greatest veneration,

your Majesty's

most obedient

most devoted, and

most humble servant,

FREDERICK,

SON OF THE LATE THEODORE, KING OF CORSICA.

DESCRIPTION

OF

CORSICA.

THE moſt conſidcrable Iſlands in the Mediterranean are, Sicily, Sardinia, and Corſica.
They make part of Italy, and have always
been deemed its ramparts; their natural
language is the Italian; they profeſs the
Catholic religion, and acknowledge the fu-
premacy of the Pope; but, being governed by
different ſovereigns they differ from each
other in their cuſtoms and laws.

Sicily holds the firſt rank, Sardinia the
ſecond, and Corſica the third.

Sicily was called by the Greeks *Trinacria*
on account of its triangular form. This

iſland

ifland is feparated from the kingdom of Naples, towards *Abruzzo*, by a fhort ftrait, which is called *Il Faro di Meffina*. Its paffage is dangerous on account of Scylla and Charybdis ; the one being a rock under water and the other a whirling abforbing vortex.

This ifland is two hundred miles long and upwards, from the *Faro* to *Capo Boço*, and one hundred and fifty-eight miles broad, from *Punta di Melazzo* to *Capo Paffaro*. It is immenfely rich in antiques, monuments, and curiofities both of art and nature.

There is a burning mountain, which the ancients called Ætna, conftantly vomiting forth bituminous fubftance. It is, however, very fingular, that its environs fhould be fmiling in verdure, and be very fertile.

Sicily, before its being fubdued by the Romans, was the nurfery of arts, belles lettres, fciences, poets, hiftorians, generals, and tyrants. The greateft, and moft cruel

of

of thofe tyrants, were Agathocles, Phalaris, and the two Dionifij, father and fon ; of whom Plutarch amply fpeaks in the lives of Dion and Timoleon. Its principal cities are, Palermo, Meffina, Catania, Agrigento, and Syracufe. Palermo is the capital, and the refidence of the Vice-roy. The nobility is ancient and numerous. There are two univerfities, Palermo and Catania; three archbifhopricks, and nine bifhopricks.

The foil is fo fertile in oil, wine, grains, and fruits, that it was called the granary of Rome.

Its air is pure and falubrious ; the inhabitants are very fober and long lived ; they are computed to amount to one million and three hundred thoufand. It abounds in cattle and game, and the fea around it is full of all forts of fifh ; the ports and havens are very commodious, and trade and commerce in a very flourifhing ftate.

B 2 Sardinia

Sardinia was called by the ancients *Ichnufa*, or *Sandalinis*, on account of its figure, which refembles the impreffion of a man's foot. It is faid that Sardus, fon of the Lybian Hercules, brought a colony to this ifland, and that he gave it the name by which it is now known. Sardina is one hundred and fifty miles in length, and ninety in breadth; there is one archbifhoprick, and feven bifhopricks; it abounds in wine, oil, grains, orange, citron trees, and other delicious fruits; it has alfo plenty of cattle and game; there are fome mines of gold, filver, lead, and copper; its fea is full of fifh; the principal and moft lucrative fifhery is that of the Coral. The air, however, is unhealthy, which is one reafon why it is not well peopled, its inhabitants amounting only to four hundred and twenty thoufand. Cagliari is its capital.

There grows an herb in this ifland of a very fingular nature. This herb refembles the *Meliffa*, and is faid to have this extraordinary.

dinary quality, that whoever fwallows the fmalleft quantity of. it is immediately deprived of his fenfes, and feized with a continual fit of laughter. It is a convulfion. The Romans called it *Rifus Sardonicus*, Sardonic Laughter; and if proper remedies are not applied in time, the patient will inevitably die laughing.

Corfica is about one hundred and fifty miles in length, fifty in breadth, and three hundred and twenty in circumference; its inhabitants amount to about one hundred and twenty thoufand; it was called by the Greeks *Cyrnos*, Therapne or Corfis, and by the Romans Corfica; it extends in length between the forty-firft and forty-third degrees of north latitude, and in breadth from twenty-fix degrees` ten minutes to twenty-feven degrees fifteen minutes eaft longitude.

It has the republic of Genoa to the north, the ecclefiaftical patrimony to the eaft, the ifland of Sardinia (from which it is feparated by a ftrait of nine miles broad) to the fouth, and the fea of Provence to the weft.

It

It is divided in two parts; namely *Banda di dentro* and *Banda di fuori*, or ·*di quá dai monti* and *di lá dai monti*. Baſtia is the capital of that part called *di quá dai monti*, this ſide of the mountains; and Ajaccio of that part called *di lá dai monti*, beyond the mountains.

Theſe diviſions are again ſubdivided into juriſdictions; theſe into pieves, or pariſhes, and the latter into villages.

The country is mountainous and rocky, the climate temperate, the ſoil fertile, but the air is remarkably unhealthy.

It contains immenſe foreſts of trees of different kinds; ſuch as oaks, holmy oaks, pines, firs, corks, beeches, aſhes, cheſnuts, walnuts, figs, oranges, citrons, and many others.

It is from Corſican oaks that the Genoeſe uſed to build their ſhips, and thoſe which they diſpoſed of to other European powers. Many of the French ſhips of war were built at Genoa with Corſican timber.

Its productions confist in wine, oil, corn, legumes, wax, honey, and various fruits of the delicious kind.

Corfican honey is not fo fweet as that which is made in other countries; it is bitterifh, or tartifh, termed in Italian *agro dolce*. The reafon of its bitternefs is, becaufe the bees feed upon the flowers of box-wood, with which this ifland abounds. The natives think that this honey contributes to longevity; they therefore eat of it frequently, and in large quantities.

In this ifland there is a vaft number of mulberry-trees, the leaves of which, when tender, ferve as food to filk worms. This wonderful infect is like a caterpillar, undergoes four changes, and at laft comes out of the cod like a butterfly, with four wings and feveral feet. Its original is from China, the beft ordered, the beft cultivated, the moft fertile, and the moft abundant part of the known world. That country fupplies Europe with many delicious things, which nature has denied to this hemifphere. It

B 4   is

is much to be lamented, that its political
fyftem has not yet reached this part of the
globe; for there is great reafon to believe
that it is more folid and rational than any
other in Europe, as it has fubfifted in its
original purity more than four thoufand
years fince its firft inftitution, without having undergone the leaft alteration in any
of its laws, manners, language, or even
mode of clothing, a ftrong proof of its perfection; which is ftill farther confirmed by
the behaviour of the Tartars Mancheux,
who, after having conquered that vaft empire in the year 1644, fubmitted themfelves
to the laws, cuftoms, and religion of the
people they had fubdued. It were to be
wifhed, therefore, that we had an ample
and perfect account of the Chinefe legifla-
ture; of which to this day, we have fome
fragments only; for furely nothing can be
more ufeful, and even more neceffary, to a
Prince, than a full knowledge of the laws of
foreign countries, which would enable him
to difcern what was good or bad in each,
and teach hi.x how to prevent or reform the
abufes

abufes which might creep into the police, the judicature, the adminiftration of
finances, the military difcipline, and all the
other parts of his own government. To return to the point: The infect in queftion
paffed from China into Perfia and from
thence into Europe. It is from Corfican filk
that the Genoefe fabricate the greateft part
of their damafks and velvets. The French
alfo ufe a great quantity in their manufac-
tures at Lyons.

This ifland has many rivers. The moft
confiderable are the *Guelo* and the *Tavignano*.
It is watered befides by a number of fprings
and rivulets, that give it a pleafing verdure,
and make it very agreeable to the eye. Its
waters are very clear, light, uncommonly
wholefome, and grateful to the palate.

There is a lake called *Il ftagno di Diana*;
in which the falt is found without any procefs, merely by the heat of the fun; and in
the jurifdiction of Vico there are mineral
waters.

On

On mount Gradaccio there are two lakes,
called *Creno* and *Ino*, at fome diftance from
each other. The waters of the firft are foapy,
and fo hot, that, upon throwing a dog,
or cat, or any other fmall animal, into them,
and letting it remain fome time, the flefh
comes off the bones, and leaves only a
fkeleton.

The water of the fecond is fo cold, that if
a bottle of red wine be immerfed in it, for a
few minutes, the liquor lofes its colour, as
well as its tafte, and affumes the qualities of
the water.

Towards the middle of the ifland is a
rivulet, called *Reftonica*, a pretended corrup-
tion of the Latin words, *res unica*. Its waters
have indeed a very remarkable quality : If a
piece of wood be left in it for a few hours, it
becomes quite white. The ruftieft iron, under
the fame circumftances, will foon appear as
if it were filvered. Its waters are very
wholefome; the natives find it as a fpecific
for the dropfy

There are mines of iron, lead, copper, and filver; quarries of marble of different colours; falines, and beds of faltpetre.

On fome mountains is found a kind of rock-cryftal, which is very tranfparent, and fo hard, that it will ftrike fire againft fteel. The Corficans generally ufe it as flints to their fire arms. It is very remarkable, that every piece of this cryftal has naturally five fides, as if it had been regularly cut by a lapidary.

The land is ploughed by oxen; thefe are fmall, and not in great number. The Corficans make no other ufe of them than that juft mentioned, as they feldom eat beef, preferring mutton or goat's flefh to it.

Almoft all the mountains, excepting fome of the higheft, which are rocks buried in fnow, are covered with a light fandy earth, which is abundantly fertile when cultivated.

Between thefe mountains are fituated the moft pleafing valleys, which might be rendered

dered by cultivation extremely fruitful, moft of them being watered by rivers or fmaller ftreams, whofe courfe might be eafily diverted, as all thefe valleys have declivities, along which ferpentine brooks might convey the winding waters at pleafure.

The pafturage is rich, and in great plenty, affording fubfiftence to numbers of cattle, and particularly to fheep. Thefe are almoft all black, their wool, however, is very fine.

Their flocks are never houfed, but are kept on the mountains, where they find fufficient pafture from the beginning of May to the month of October. At the approach of winter they are driven into the valleys, where it never fnows, and where they find alfo fufficient fuftenance, particularly in the declivities of the mountains bordering on the fea. The fhepherds build themfelves occafional huts with the branches of trees, which they cover with ftraw, and in which they refide with their wives and children. They fubfift chiefly on milk diet,

are

are emigrants that have no fixed habitations, nor belong to any particular parish.

There is also a prodigious number of *16-*swine; they are all black like the wild boars, and for the most part of a mixed breed.

Poultry and game are in the greatest plenty. There are no wolves, nor rabbits, but a great number of foxes.

There is a wild animal resembling a goat, which the Corsicans call *Muffoli*. This creature is so nimble, that it springs from one rock to another at an amazing distance, and is generally taken in a snare. By a strange singularity, however, he attaches himself to the first person that spits into his mouth, and ever after follows him up and down like a spaniel.

There are mules, and horses, both of a small size, but well made and strong. The horses are spirited, and extremely sure-footed, traversing the most difficult moun-

tains

tains without being fhod, and running over
ftones without ftumbling.

The dogs are large, fierce, and treacherous, and fo ftrong that they fet upon the
wild boars, and overpower them.

According to Pliny, there were formerly
no lefs than three and thirty towns .in the
ifland, but at this time there are only nine :
thefe are *Baftia, San Fiorenzo, Calvi, Ajaccio, Bonifacio, Porto Vecchio, Aleria, Mariana*, and *Corte*. Thefe towns never had
any other fortification, or fences, but thofe
which common fenfe fuggefted before the
ufing of artillery; that is to fay a ditch, a
rampart wall, and tower.

The whole coaft of this ifland is full of
gulfs, and harbours, or havens. The havens
of San Fiorenzo, of Calvi, of Porto, of Sagone, of Ajaccio, of Valinco, of Bonifacio,
and of Porto Vecchio are the beft.

There are befides other fmall harbours,
which the Corficans call *Calles*, and thefe

are

are that of Algajola, of Giralatte, of Figaro, and many others of this kind, where small veffels can enter with fafety.

Baftia is the largeft town, and is well peopled. It contains about five thoufand inhabitants. It is built on the declivity of a mountain, and its inequalities render it very inconvenient. The ftreets are badly paved and very narrow. Its inhabitants are looked upon to be good mariners. Formerly they practifed piracy. Its port is fmall and the entrance dangerous on account of rocks at the mouth of it. The port as well as the own is commanded by a citadel, which, however, is indifferently fortified.

San Fiorenzo has upwards of one hundred houfes. The air is unwholefome, but the harbour, or rather the haven, is commodious, and fafe.

Calvi is more confiderable. It contains upwards of two hundred and forty houfes. Its citadel is very ftrong both by nature and art,

art, and the harbour better than that of San Fiorenzo.

Sagone was formerly a well peopled town, and the feat of a bifhop, at prefent it exifts no more. There is, however, a good port.

Ajaccio is the fineft town in the whole ifland, and the beft fituated. This town together with its jurifdiction contains four thoufand fix hundred and fifty families. The houfes are well built, the ftreets ftrait and well paved, and the fuburbs embellifhed with beautiful buildings. There are fine walks on the right and the left of the town, towards the fea, as well as on the mole, which is an excellent one. Its harbour, or rather its gulf, is the fafeft, the largeft and the moft commodious in the whole ifland. There is a rock before the mole which could eafily be mined and fprung in the month of February, or March, when the fea is low. If this were done the largeft fhips might anchor with fafety near the mole. Its citadel is regularly fortified, but cannot make a long refiftance.

In

In this gulf there is a fifhery of coral, which is of three forts, red, white, and black.

The harbour of Valinco, though not fo fpacious as that of Ajaccio, is neverthelefs equally fafe and commodious.

Bonifacio is fituated in the fouthern part of the ifland towards Sardinia, and is feparated from it by a narrow ftrait of nine miles. Here is a very good harbour, and a ftrong caftle. The town contains about five hundred families, who are extremely induftrious. In this gulf there is alfo a fifhery of coral.

Porto Vecchio was formerly a very confiderable town, but is now quite deferted, on account of the bad air occafioned by fwamps. Here are not above feventy families. The harbour, however, is fafe.

Aleria and Mariana labour under the fame inconvenience, thefe two towns being

C   very

very thinly inhabited on account of their unwholefomenefs.

Corte is fituated almoft in the centre of the ifland. It is furrounded by inacceffible mountains. There is a good old caftle. The town and its jurifdiction contains upwards of three thoufand families.

For the thorough fatisfaction of the reader, we have inferted at the end of this work a correct ftatement of the population of the whole ifland.

There are five bifhopricks, namely, that of Ajaccio, Calvi, Aleria, Bonifacio, and Nebbio. This latter has undergone the ravages of time. It is reduced at prefent to a heap of ruins. Its bifhop refides at Baftia.

Corfica fwarms with priefts and monks, the greateft part of whom are of mean fentiments, and extremely ignorant; they are held, neverthelefs, in great veneration by the common people, as their teachers and directors,

directors, in point of religion, are received every where with open arms, and regarded as masters of the house *Padroni di Casa.* These ecclesiasticks are as turbulent, and as seditious as the seculars. They have been the firebrands of every revolution that has happened in that country, and have encouraged the people to take up arms against their sovereign.

There is a Greek colony, which has been established in that island ever since the year one thousand six hundred and seventy-six. They are the descendants of those ancient Spartans, whose actions and manner of speaking all nations have admired, but no one ever has imitated. They were virtuous from principle, honour, and emulation. Patriotism, courage, firmness, sobriety, and the military science, constituted their character truly manly ; in so much, that Diogenes, the cynic, coming from Sparta, and going to Corinth, being asked whence he came ? replied " That he was coming from " a country inhabited by men, and was go-

C 2   " ing

" ing to one inhabited by women." In fact,
Sparta has given the world a number of
very great men, particularly in the art of
war. From them we have many maxims,
regulations, and manœuvres, which Generals make ufe of to this day. To them we
owe the evolutions which a corps makes in
order to keep its ground, or to gain another,
namely the fquare, thereby being able to
face the enemy on every fide. We owe alfo
to them the attack in column, and feveral
other evolutions, the detail of which would
lead us too far from our prefent undertaking.
We fhall only fay, That Philip, King of
Macedonia, and his fon Alexander the Great,
though they bore a mortal enmity to the
Lacedemonians, and found fault with every
thing they did, yet they preferred the Spartan evolutions to the Macedonians, and practifed them to advantage in their conquefts.
Several of thofe evolutions have been elu-
cidated, and inculcated by the Chevalier Fo-
lard, and the late King of Pruffia adopted
them with fuccefs in fome of the battles
which he fought with the Auftrians.

The

The Lacedemonians did not confine themfelves to precepts only. They invented alfo
fome arms, among which was a fingular
fword. This fword was fhort and crooked
like a fcythe. They faid, that it fhould be
fhort for people like themfelves, who de-
fired to clofe with the enemy; upon which
Archilogus faid,

" Slings they defpife, and fcorn to fend from far,
" The flying dart, and wage a diftant war,
" But hand to hand the trufty fword they wield,
" Do all the dreadful bufinefs of the field."

Their whole life was employed in ftudy-
ing how to die glorioufly. Other nations
ran to victory when it was almoft certain, but
the Lacedemonians ran to death even when
they were fure of it. " It is very fhameful,"
Seneca faid, " for any man to run away, but
" it would be unpardonable in a Spartan
" even to think of it." They were fo de-
licate on that point, that they banifhed Archilogus from Sparta for faying in jeft, " That
" it would be wifer to run away than to
" fall fword in hand," they maintaining

C 3   that

that the courageous ought to fave themfelves
by their hands, fighting till they either get
the victory or fall in the combat, whilft pol-
troons will fave themfelves by their legs.

As long as the Spartans religioufly obferved the wife inftitutions of Lycurgus,
they were invincible, but as foon as they
neglected them, and beftowed their time,
labour, and induftry, upon corrupting themfelves by ignoble pleafures, diffipations, and
riots, they loft the pre-eminence which they
had held over Greece, were defeated by Pe-
lopidas and Epaminondas, afterwards were
fubdued by Philip, King of Macedonia, then
by the Romans, and at laft enflaved by the
Turks, in the year 1460. Thefe barbarians
overturned and deftroyed every veftige of
that illuftrious nation, and now the en-
quiring traveller can find nothing but the
barren fpot where Sparta ftood.

After that period, the Lacedemonians
began to emigrate; and the colony we
are fpeaking of, landed in Corfica in the

I   year

year 1676. They preferred this ifland to any other habitation more agreeably fitu-ated, merely becaufe being mountainous and rough, it prefented them with the image of their native country.

The Republic of Genoa granted them fome large tracts of land, which had not been cul-tivated for many centuries. The want of culture is the reafon why Corfica has al-ways been confidered as fterile and unpro-ductive. Thofe tracts of land were called *Paonia, Revida,* and *Salogna.* They efta-blifhed themfelves in *Paonia,* where they built five villages; namely, *Salico, Corona, Paucone, Rondellino,* and *Monte Roffo.* They cultivated it fo well, that in a fhort time it afforded them all the comforts of life. But the Corficans, growing envious of the pro-fperity of thefe new fettlers, rofe in a mafs, and deftroyed their fettlements. There is a certain depravity in fome men which in-duces them to injure others without any benefit to themfelves. Thofe induftrious emigrants, unwilling to expofe themfelves

C 4   to

to further injuries and loffes, abandoned agriculture, and retired to Ajaccio. Ufed to viciffitudes, they were no ways dejected. Recollecting their origin, they refumed their ancient military inftitution ; regimented themfelves for the fervice of the Republic of Genoa, and appointed *Stephanopoli* to be their commander, who was the moft re- fpectable man among them, and he difci- plined them fo well, and rendered them fo fubmiffive and obedient, and at the fame time fo bold, refolute, and daring, that they were as loth to incur blame as they were ardent to gain honour and glory ; and on all occafions fought as valiantly under him, as they would have done under the eye of Lycurgus himfelf.

Under the dependence of Corfica there is a fmall ifland, called *Capraja*, formerly belonging to the family of *de Maro*, a family once very powerful in Corfica. The dif- tance between thefe two iflands is computed to be feven or eight leagues. Capraja is but fix leagues in circumference. In ancient

times

times it was inhabited by Monks only, who had renounced all commerce with the world, had devoted themselves to prayer and abstinence, and professed celibacy, a kind of life which the wise Lycurgus and several other legiflators had forbidden, becaufe it was contrary to the dictates of nature, and deftructive to the propagation of the human fpecies. While thefe Monks, plunged in floth, inhabited this ifland, it was a heap of weeds, briars, and thorns. *Jacopo de Maro*, a man of noble and enlarged ideas drove them out of it, demolifhed their convents, and invited over men who got their fubfiftence by labour, and thefe cultivated Capraja fo well, that it produces now in plenty all forts of grain, wine, oil, and whatever elfe is neceffary for the comforts and conveniencies of life. There is a borough which contains about feven hundred inhabitants. It is protected by a ftrong caftle built upon a hill. The Republic of Genoa afterwards difpoffeffed Jacopo de Maro of that ifland, and ever fince they have kept a ftrong garrifon in it.

REVOLUTION

REVOLUTION

OF

CORSICA.

THE preceding is an accurate defcription of the fituation, clime, foil, and productions of Corfica, which notwithftanding the many gifts, it is abundantly furnifhed with by provident nature, has always been miferably poor, never having been able to fupply the neceffary expences for its civil and military eftablifhments, and having always proved a dead weight on the different fovereigns who have poffeffed it. But poverty, inftead of dejecting their fpirits, made them bold, refolute, and valiant, in fo much that whenever they found themfelves oppreffed, they readily took up arms againft their oppreffors, howfoever powerful and opulent they might be. Their invincible courage and fteady abhorrence to flavery, which they had fhown in a long feries of ftruggles, impreffed the citizen of Geneva (Rouffeau,

in

in the Social Contract) with the following
fentiment:

    " Il eſt encore en Europe un pays eapa-
" ble de legiſlation. C'eſt l'Iſle de Corſe.
" La valeur, et la conſtance, avec la quelle
" ce brave peuple a ſcu recouvrer, et de-
" fendre ſa liberté, meriteroit bien que
" quelque homme ſage lui apprit à la
" conſerver. J'ai quelque preſſentiment,
" qu'un jour cette petite iſle étcnnera
" l'Europe."

Many other eminent authors have written
alſo on the ſame ſubjeƈt, among whom was
the celebrated Mrs. Macaulay. This lady re-
commended a democratical government,
drew a ſketch of it, and addreſſed it to
Signor Paoli, the Corſican leader, who had
it in contemplation to eſtabliſh in Corſica
that form of government, and her memorable letter begins thus:

    " Warm wiſhes for the welfare of your-
" ſelf and illuſtrious countrymen, re-
" nowned Paoli! are the motives which
                          " ſtimu-

" ftimulate me to addrefs you on the
" important fubject of Corfican liberty.—
" Free eftablifhments are fubjects I have
" ftudied with care, and the ftrong rumours
" which prevail, that the Corficans are
" going to eftablifh a Republic, makes me
" addrefs you, as if this was the deter-
" mined point to which your views are
" turned."

Mrs. Macauley, after laying down the
rules which fhe thought efficient for fuch an
eftablifhment, concludes her letter in the
following words :

" That there was no perfon fo capable
" for this high employment as Signor Paoli,
" who having long directed the councils of
" a brave people in the glorious ftruggle of
" liberty, fhould finifh his career by making
" that liberty beneficial, and permanent.
" This is an opportunity of immortalizing
" your name, renowned Paoli ! which few
" men have had within their power, and
" fewer have had wifdom enough to feize
" on, but rather through their folly have
                                    " turned

" turned it to difgrace and infamy. But
" that you may be ranked among the fore-
" moſt of mortals with Timoleon, Lycur-
" gus, Solon, and Brutus, is the ſincere
" wiſh of your great admirer,
        " and very humble fervant,
            " CATHERINE MACAULAY."

After this addreſs, ſo flattering to Paoli,
it may not be improper to give the reader
ſome account of his origin, his education,
and talents, and how he came to be the firſt
man in authority and power in that iſland.

His Chriſtian name is Paſqual, and Giacinto was that of his father. Giacinto Paoli
was created Marquis, by King Theodore,
who appointed him afterwards his High
Treaſurer, and on that Monarch's departure
from Corſica was a member of the Regency.
Paſqual Paoli was educated at Naples under
the Jeſuits. He made a great progreſs in
the different branches of polite literature, as
well as in their ſyſtem of politics, learning
with avidity the latent precepts of advanc-
ing in life, and the art of managing mens'
                                    tempers

tempers and paffions. He was active and
fober, never indulging idlenefs, or abandoning himfelf to the grofs pleafures of fenfu-
ality, which not only enervate the vigor
and the ftrength of the body, but blunt the
acutenefs of every faculty of the mind;
with thefe fingular advantages and a great
fagacity and penetration, Paoli from Naples went to Corfica among rude and un-
couth people, who were ftrangers to
thofe mental embellifhments, and to political intrigues, but who were cut out for the
executive bufinefs of war, and wholly given
to recover their liberty by a ftubborn courage. He officiated at firft as Secretary to
Doctor Caffori, a phyfician, and his kinf-
man, who was at the head of the mal-
contents. Caffori was affaffinated, and
Paoli ftrove to attain the high poft which
the deceafed had occupied. But he met
with a powerful opponent in the perfon
of *Signor Matra,* who being a man of
noble fentiments, a true lover of his country, and a brave and experienced warrior,
thought himfelf entitled to mount to a degree

gree of eminence above the reſt, and have the command of his armed countrymen preferably to Paoli. Force, and not the number of votes, was to decide the conteſt. The two parties armed their reſpective partizans and came to blows. The Paoliſts were defeated; and Paoli, thinking himſelf in danger of his life, took ſanctuary in a convent together with ſome of his friends, where they were cloſely blockaded. But *Matra* met with the ſame fate as Caffori, and his tragical death was an object of triumph and joy to Paoli, who being now releaſed from fear, ruſhed out of the convent, ſet at work all the engines of his politicks, and by plauſible ſpeeches and ample promiſes prevailed upon the multitude to chuſe him for their General.

He now had the ſole government of their civil and military affairs, and gained ſuch an aſcendancy and dominion over them, that they implicitly aſſented to every thing he propoſed, abandoning the care of their moſt important concerns to his diſcretion, and magnifying him as a man of the greateſt truſt and command.

Paoli's

Paoli's patrimony was but slender: it consisted in a house and a garden which he had at *Rostino*, where he was born. The Corsicans plentifully supplied him with what he wanted, and raised that provision by an annual tax, which was called *Il pane del Generale*, the General's bread.

As he was not trained up to arms, a profession of an indispensable necessity to a man who is engaged in military enterprises, he could not possibly drive the Genoese out of Corsica. These, nevertheless, despairing to subdue them, in the year 1768, resigned the sovereignty of that Island to Louis XV, King of France, who paid to that Republick forty millions of livres for it. Besides that sum, the expences annually incurred for the support of its civil and military establishments, have amounted to nine hundred thousand livres, as it is stated in the annexed memoirs which were presented to the French National Assembly in the year 1790, on the exploitation, or felling of the woods in that island; a plan calculated to relieve the French Treasury of those

D   expences,

expences, create an income, without im-
pofing any tax on the inhabitants, and promote induftry and occupations among the
common people.

Paoli did not feem difmayed by this cef-
fion ; on the contrary, he animated the Corficans to perfevere in the defence of their
liberty, which, including every other blef-
fing, is therefore the only thing worth con-
tending for to the laft ; and he promifed to
ftand by, or fall with them.

This heroic refolution being fpread
about all over Italy, and afterwards all over
Europe, gained him the efteem and good
wifhes of every lover of humanity, and the
affiftance of the wealthy, who fupplied him
with arms, ammunition, and money. On
that occafion *Buttafuoco*, and *Colonna*, two
Corfican gentlemen who had ferved with
diftinction in the Corfican regiment in the
fervice of France, and likewife the author
of this narrative, who had made feveral
campaigns under the moft experienced Generals of the age, and had feen a variety of
war, offered to join Paoli in fo glorious a
caufe,

caufe, but he rejected their offer. Mighty doings were expected from his valour and conduct, particularly here in England, where he was ftiled the Corfican Timoleon.

But Paoli did not fulfil his promifes to the Corficans, nor juftified the general opinion which had been entertained of him. At the appearance of the French troops, he ftole away in the hour of danger, abandoning his countrymen as a prey to their enemies, and took with him the donations which had been fo liberally fubfcribed here in London under the direction and truft of Alderman Beckford, Alderman Trecothick, and Samuel Vaughan, Efq; for the relief of thofe brave defenders of their liberty ; which donations he had received but three days before his precipitate retreat. This action brought upon him the odium of every man of honourable fentiments, and the indignation of thofe gentlemen. But on his arrival in London, his fubmiffive letters, friendly interpofitions in behalf of the penitent, and their humane difpofition, converted indignation into mercy.

Notwith-

Notwithftanding thefe heavy charges, which muft have been unknown at St. James's, or looked upon as calumnious, Paoli was prefented to the King, was gracioufly received, and gratified with a large penfion. He obtained, befides, a provifion for *Signor Clemente*, his brother, another for *Signor Barbaggio*, his nephew, and for feveral others who had followed his fortune.

Thefe diftinguifhed marks of royal favour operated as his regeneration, wiping off the odium of his flight, and reconciling him to the Corficans, who now took that flight for a political manœuvre, and a preconcerted plan with the Englifh Government; and they were given to underftand, that the King being the reprefentative of a free nation, would at a proper time efpoufe their caufe, enable them to fhake off the yoke of an arbitrary Prince, and to become an independent Commonwealth, which though a poor one, they preferred it to a golden fervitude, as fetters of gold are fetters ftill; Paoli therefore bid them to be of good heart, and kept alive in them the divine flame of liberty.

4

But

But by little and little he abandoned the republican principles, and became a devotee to kingly government; infomuch, that when the prefent moft fudden, moft un-expected, and moft aftonifhing revolution broke out in France, and that nation over-turned the royal throne, declared themfelves a free people, infpired the furrounding na-tions with the fame fentiments, gave li-berty to Corfica, and affiliated her as one of the fections, Paoli fhewed a great concern at this change in his country. As foon as, however, the emotions of his mind fub-fided, he wrote a letter to his countrymen, which appeared in the newfpapers, con-gratulating them on the recovery of their liberty, but lamenting that as Corfica, ne-verthelefs, made part of France, he could not join them confiftently with the princi-ples of gratitude, and his attachment to the Englifh nation, from whom he had long received, and was actually receiving great favours.

Sometime after he left England, went to Paris, pleaded and obtained his pardon, pro-pounced an oration at the bar of the affem-

bly;

bly; in which he faid, that after a painful
exile of twenty years, he felt it now the
happieft moment of his life to fee liberty
reftored to his country by the generofity of
the French nation, and expreffed his earneft
defire and readinefs to contribute, as far as
it was in his power, to the happinefs of his
fellow-citizens. Thefe fentiments being
the nobleft that ever animated human heart,
were highly pleafing to the national affembly, and met with an univerfal applaufe.
Accordingly he took the oath of fidelity,
was reinftated to his former command, and
embarked for his native country, where he
was received with the ftrongeft marks of
acclamation. And now it was thought
that Corfica, after being long toffed up and
down, like a fhip in the wide fea by
tempeftuous weather, having now happily
reached a good port, would reft enjoying
a ferene calm, and no more venture on
defperate enterprifes. But the contrary
happened; Paoli began to undermine the
eftablifhed form of government, and to
poifon the mind of the people againft the
French nation.

The

The convention being informed of his
fecret practices, and of each particular of his
defigns, ordered him to appear at their bar,
and exhibit himfelf to juftice on what had
been alleged againft him. Age and infirmities
were the reafons he gave that he might be
difpenfed from appearing; and he accompanied thefe reafons with affurances that
he would never be defective to his duty.
But he ftill going on in caballing, was fum-
moned again, and as he peremptorily re-
fufed to obey, (thinking himfelf fafe at
Corte, an inland town of very difficult accefs, fituated in the centre of the ifle) the
convention declared him a traitor, and fet
a price upon his head.

The French had not above four hundred
men of their own nation in that ifland, and
thefe were diftributed in garrifoning Baftia,
San Fiorenzo, and Calvi, places fituated on
the fea fide, the command of which was
intrufted to native Corficans. As mutual
confidence reigned between the mother
country and the affiliated, no greater number of troops was thought neceffary to be
fent over for each others fecurity and to main-

tain

tain order. But Paoli availing himfelf of
the paucity of the French troops, of the
credit he had with his countrymen, naturally
turbulent, and lovers of change, and the
hope of receiving a powerful fuccour from
England, openly excited a revolt, with a
view to add his mite to the efforts of this
nation against the convention, then confidered as a motley crew, and of no con-
fiftence, fave his own life, and gratify his
ambition for power.

His defection difunited two nations,
who feemed faftened to one another with
an indiffoluble knot, and converted the
tranquillity of Corfica into a violent fer-
mentation. Thofe iflanders, agitated by
different motives and paffions, formed
themfelves into two different parties.

One of thofe parties was headed by
Gentili, Saliceti, Arena, Cafa Bianca, and
many other gentlemen of the firft families
and fortune in that ifland, who thought it
unjuft, and abfurd to depart, without caufe,
from a conftitution, the obfervance of which
they had fworn to, in the prefence of the

Supreme

Supreme Being, whom they called for witnefs, and from which they had actually derived fignal advantages; they fided, therefore, with the convention, who preached a doctrine congenial to their own fentiments, namely, liberty, equality, and fraternity, and fupport that doctrine with an enthufiafm, which nothing can refift, and from which no difficulties can deter them.

At the head of the other party was General Paoli, encompaffed and fupported by the clergy, whom he had inftigated to rife againft the convention for intending to apply to the neceffary expences of the ftate, part of the annual revenues of the church, for annulling her inftitutions and rites, vilifying the relicks and images of the faints, overturning their altars, and profaning the temples. This party was denominated the *Sacred Band*, and all true believers were commanded to take up arms in order to avenge fo holy a caufe.

This party was more numerous than the other, and acquired an additional ftrength by Paoli's fecretly inviting over the Englifh
fleet,

fleet, which, after the hasty evacuation of Toulon, and the Republic of Genoa refusing to admit them into their harbours, wandered about in those seas for want of a proper shelter. Them the *Sacred Band* received as their deliverers from tyranny, and the protectors of their Roman Catholic religion.

The sudden and unexpected arrival of this formidable armament disconcerted the Corsican democrats, who were not prepared for such an event. Thus being unable to keep their ground, and averse to infest their country with the horrors of a civil war, and imbrue their hands in the blood of their fellow-citizens, they desisted for the present from supporting the established government. They calmly separated, and some of them retired to Bastia, some to San Fiorenzo, some to Calvi, where the French republic had a garrison, repeating in their journey the following lines of an ancient poet—

Where-ever discord, and rebellion reign,
The worst of men, the greatest honors gain.

Others

Others remained quiet in their own habitations, without interfering in public matters, as they were of opinion that the rebels would foon be fenfible of their error, would correct their offence by repentance, and turn enemies to the authors of that rebellion. ' And others knowing that Paoli was formed on the principles of Machiavel, who prefcribes to *kill* your enemy, if you cannot make him your friend, being now in the plenitude of an abfolute power, were apprehenfive he would facrifice them to his vengeance; they therefore joined him, and affented to whatever he propofed. Befides the inducement of the fafety of their perfons and property, they expected to fhare equally with his friends, the private emoluments and numerous employments which he had promifed them in the name of a very potent and very liberal monarch, replete with virtues, and juft to his promife. Accordingly after the furrender of Baftia, San Fiorenzo, and Calvi to the Englifh forces, and Corfica, by the reduction of thofe places, being entirely clear of French troops, Paoli convoked a General Affembly at Corte, and being attired in the ve-
nerable

nerable titles of patriot, and a benefactor to his beloved countrymen, in the moſt ſolemn manner ſurrendered their liberties to the king of Great-Britain, and com- mitted, at the ſame time, the care and protection of the Roman Catholic religion to that monarch, though a Proteſtant.

The form and condition of which are fully related in the following

STATE PAPERS:

To the Right Honourable Henry Dundas.

SIR,

I have the honour to acquaint you, that the union of Corſica to the Crown of Great Britain is finally and formally concluded; and it is with the moſt ſincere ſatisfaction that I find myſelf enabled to aſſure you, that no national act was ever ſanctioned by a more unanimous proceeding on the part of thoſe who were authoriſed to do it, or by a more univerſal approbation, amounting, I may ſay, to enthuſiaſm, on the part of the people.

I have

I have already had the honour of tranfmit-
ting to you a copy of the letter addreffed
by His Excellency my Lord Hood and
myfelf to His Excellency General Paoli,
dated the 21ft of April. I have the honour
to inclofe, to-day, a copy of the Circular
Letter, addreffed by General Paoli to his
countrymen, referring to that which he had
received from us; an Italian tranflation of
which was annexed.

Letters of convocation were foon after
iffued for the Affembly of the General Confult, to be held at Corté, on Sunday, the
8th of June; and were fo framed, as to procure the moft general reprefentation known
in this ifland; every community, which is the
fmalleft territorial divifion, having fent its
reprefentative; and the ftate of property
being fuch, that, although none but land-
holders were electors, every man almoft
without exception has voted.

The letters of convocation fet forth the
occafion of their being called together; and
the minutes of election in every community
expreffed

expreffed the general nature of the meafure to which the Deputies were authorifed to confent, fpecifying diftinctly the union of Corfica with Great Britain, and the tender of the Crown to his Majefty.

I have the honour to inclofe copies of thefe proceedings.

The Deputies met at Corté in fufficient numbers to conftitute the Affembly, on Tuefday the 10th of June. Some days were employed in verifying their powers, and determining controverted elections; after which they chofe General Paoli as their Prefident, and Mr. Pozzodi Bargo and Mr. Mufelli their Secretaries.

On Saturday, the 14th inftant, General Paoli opened the Affembly by an excellent and eloquent fpeech, ftating concifely the principal events which had occurred, and the principal meafures adopted by himfelf, fince the feparation of the laft General Confult in May 1793, the occafion of their prefent convocation,

vocation, and the leading points on which their deliberations fhould turn.

The Affembly voted unanimoufly their thanks to General Paoli, and a full and entire approbation of all he had done, by virtue of the powers formerly vefted in him by the Confult of 1793.

They then 1ft, declared unanimoufly the feparation of Corfica from France.

And, 2dly, with the fame unanimity, and with the ftrongeft demonftrations of univer- fal fatisfaction and joy, voted the union of Corfica to the Crown of Great Britain.

A Committee was then appointed to pre- pare the Articles of Union, and to confider the proper mode of tendering the Crown to His Majefty.

It was declared, that all who came fhould have voices; and, in fact, feveral perfons of
character

character and talents, who were not even Members of the Affembly, were admitted to the deliberations, and took a fhare in the difcuffions of the Committee.

The Articles underwent in the Committee a very full, free, and intelligent difcuffion ; fuch as would have done honour to any affembly of public men in any country, and fuch as ftamped the refult with the fanction of a deliberate and informed, as well as a free and independent affent.

The report was voted with unanimity in the Committee.

It was prefented to the Affembly on Thurfday the 17th; and on that and the following day was opened, and moft ably, as well as fully, expounded to them by Mr. Pozzo de Bargo. It was adopted with unanimity, and with univerfal applaufe; and two copies of the Act of Union were figned by every Member of the Confult.

On

On Thurfday, the 19th of June, I received a deputation from the Affembly, prefenting to me a copy of the Act of Union, and inviting me to return with them, that the Crown might be tendered to His Majefty by the Affembly itfelf, in the moft folemn and authentic form.

I accompanied the deputation; and, in the prefence of the Affembly, received from the Prefident, His Excellency General Paoli, in the name of the people, the tender of the Crown and Sovereignty of Corfica to His Majefty.

His Excellency's addrefs to me is contained in the minutes.

After addreffing the Affembly in a manner which appeared to me fuitable to the occafion, I pronounced, in His Majefty's name, the acceptation of the Crown, according to the Articles contained in the Act of Union.

I then

I then took, in His Majefty's name, the oath prefcribed " To maintain the Liber- " ties of Corfica according to the Conftitu- " tion and the Laws."

The Prefident then took and adminiftered to the Affembly the oath of allegiance and fidelity ; after which I figned and fealed the acceptation annexed to both copies of the Act of Union, one of which I have now the honour to tranfmit,

The day following (yefterday) *Te Deum* was fung in the Cathedral, accompanied by the difcharge of artillery ; and prayers were offered up for His Majefty, by the name of George the Third, King of Great Britain and Corfica. In the evening the town was illuminated, and the people demonftrated their loyalty and joy by every means in their power.

The Affembly has voted, this day, an Addrefs to His Majefty, expreffive of their gratitude, loyalty, and attachment ; and have

have deputed four refpectable gentlemen to
prefent it to His Majefty in London.

I cannot conclude this difpatch without
offering my very humble congratulations on
the fortunate termination of this important
and interefting affair, at once advantageous,
as I truft, to the contracting parties, honour-.
able to His Majefty, and gratifying, in
every view, to his royal feelings, as well as
to thofe of His Britifh fubjects.

The true foundation and bafis of this
tranfaction has refted on the confidence infpired by his Majefty's princely virtues, and the
exalted reputation enjoyed throughout the
world by the Britifh nation for every honourable and generous quality. The people of
Corfica have, on one hand, done homage to
thofe virtues, by confiding and tendering,
even folicitoufly, the fovereignty of their
country to His Majefty; they have, on the
other hand, heightened the value of that
confidence, by evincing that it comes from

E   men

men who have rejected, with horror, the poifonous and counterfeit liberty of France, without being ignorant or carelefs of a well-ordered and conftitutional freedom.

His Majefty has acquired a crown; thofe who beftow it have acquired liberty. The Britifh nation has extended its political and commercial fphere by the acceffion of Corfica; Corfica has added new fecurities to her ancient poffeffions, and has opened frefh fields of profperity and wealth, by her liberal incorporation with a vaft and powerful empire.

This difpatch will be delivered to you by Mr. Petriconi, a young gentleman of this country, who has ferved with diftinction through-out the war, under the orders of General Paoli, and particularly in the fieges of Baftia and St. Fiorenzo.

I beg leave to refer to him for any particulars which I may have omitted, and to recommend

mend him to the honour of your attention during his refidence in England.

I have the honour to be, &c.

(Signed)   GILBERT ELLIOTT.

——

TRANSLATION.

General Paoli to his Countrymen.

Furiani, May 1, 1794.

Moft dearly-beloved Countrymen,

THE unabated confidence with which you have honoured me, and the folicitude I have had to promote your interefts, and to enfure your liberty, prefcribe to me the obligation of ftating to you the prefent fituation of public affairs.

You remember how many cruel and treacherous arrangements were made by

E 2   the

the three Commiffioners of the French
Convention, who were fent over to our
ifland; and in what manner they attempted
to concentrate the powers of government in
a fmall number of their fatellites, deftined to
be the inftruments of thofe violences and
cruelties, which were to be exercifed againft
all well-meaning perfons, and againft the
nation at large.

The unjuft decree which ordered my arreft, and my transfer to the bar of the Affembly, was the firft attempt directed by them
againft your liberty. You unanimoufly declared yourfelves, and humbly remonftrated
againft an act defigned to facilitate the execution of your enemy's plots: Finally, you,
in a General Affembly, declared your indignation at this act of injuftice; and you
adopted, at that moment, fuch refolutions,
as were confiftent with your dignity, and
with the public welfare.

J accepted, as a diftinguifhing proof of your
confidence, the commiffion you were pleafed

to confer upon me, for providing, in thofe
critical circumftances, for the maintainance of
your fafety and liberty : Anxious that you
fhould not be expofed to any danger, unlefs
indignation and neceffity commanded you to
refift, I tried every means which prudence
and moderation fuggefted to me at that
time ; but neither your juft reclamations,
nor my innocence, were fufficient to recall
to fentiments of rectitude and humanity a
violent and fanguinary faction, irritated by
the noble refiftance you had made, and re-
folved to accomplifh your deftruction ; for
which purpofe the fubverfion of the government was ordered, and the members of it
profcribed conjointly with many other zealous patriots : The nation was declared in a
ftate of rebellion ; orders were given to reduce it by force of arms, and to treat it with
the bloody rigour of revolutionary laws.

Roufed by thefe caufes, by the endlefs
fucceffion of deftruction and ruin which
characterizes the conduct of thofe perfons
who exercife the powers of government in

France,

France, and by the deſtruction of all religion, and of every form of worſhip, enforced
and proclaimed among the people with un-
exampled impiety, every Corſican felt the
neceſſity of ſeparating from the French, and
of guarding againſt the poiſonous influence
of their errors.

The acts of hoſtility committed by the
French, and thoſe Corſican traitors who had
taken refuge in the garriſons of Calvi, St.
Fiorenzo, and Baſtia, compelled us to repel
them by force of arms. I have ſeen, with
infinite ſatisfaction, during the courſe of a
whole year, that your ancient bravery and
attachment to your country were not in the
leaſt diminiſhed; in various encounters the
enemy have been defeated, although numerous and ſupported by artillery; you have
treated the priſoners taken in the heat of
battle with generoſity, whilſt the enemy
have, in cold blood, maſſacred our priſoners,
who were ſo unfortunate as to fall into their
hands. In all theſe agitations we have kept
ourſelves united, and exempt from the horrors

rors of licentioufnefs and anarchy; a happy
prefage of your future fate, and an irrefragable
proof that you are deferving of true liberty,
and that you will know how to preferve it
unfullied by licentioufnefs and diffentions.

In fuch a ftate of things, a becoming dif-
fidence made me, neverthelefs, apprehend
that the enemy would increafe in force, and
attempt to carry into execution the deftructive plans they had formed againft you.
Under thefe circumftances I felt the neceffity of foreign affiftance; and, in conformity to your general wifhes, and to the public opinion and univerfal expectation, I had
recourfe to the King, and to the generous
and powerful nation, which had, on other
occafions, protected the remains of our liberty; a meafure dictated by the public
fafety, and which I took only when every
conciliatory offer had been obftinately rejected, and every hope of obtaining moderation or juftice from the French Convention was extinct.

His

His Britannick Majefty's arms have made their appearance in your fupport; His fhips and troops are employed with you to drive from our country the common enemy; and the blood of Britons and Corficans is conjointly fhed for the liberty of this ifland. Our enterprife has already been crowned with happy events, and draws near to a fortunate completion.

This pleafing afpect of affairs has determined me to turn my thoughts to the moft efficacious means of eftablifhing a permanent freedom, and of fecuring our iflands from the various events, which, till this moment, have kept us in agitation.

The protection of the King of Great Britain, and a political union with the Britifh nation, of which the profperity and power, uninterrupted for ages, are to the univerfe proofs of the excellency of its government, have appeared to me to accord with the happinefs and fafety of Corfica. The univerfal opinion on this head, evinced

by

by the unreferved inclination you have
fhewn, and ftrengthened by your gratitude
for benefits received, appears fortunately
to concur with mine. I have, therefore,
made the proper overtures to His Majefty,
the King of Great Britain, with a view to
eftablifh this defirable Union.

With a fatisfaction, never to be erafed
from my mind, I now behold our wifhes
anticipated, and our hopes realized. The
Memorial which has been tranfmitted to me
by their Excellencies, the Admiral, com-
manding the fleet, and the Minifter Plenipotentiary of His Majefty, affords us the
opportunity of eftablifhing this Union in
the manner beft adapted to the benefit of
both Nations, and to the honour of His
Majefty. I cannot better make known to
you their Excellencies fentiments than by a
faithful tranflation of their Memorial.

The nature of the prefent Addrefs does
not permit me to enlarge upon the benefits
of this Union, which tends to conciliate the
moft

moſt extenſive political and civil liberty
with perſonal ſecurity. You are convinced
of theſe truths, and will regulate your conduct accordingly. I neverthelefs avail myfelf of this opportunity to declare to you,
that, in taking the Engliſh Conſtitution for
your model, you will proceed upon the moſt
ſolid principles, that philoſophy, policy and
experience, have ever been known to combine for the happineſs of a great people,
referving to yourſelves the power of adapt-
ing them to your own peculiar ſituation,
cuſtoms, and religion, without being ex-
poſed hereafter to the venality of a Traitor,
or to the ambition of a powerful Uſurper.

A matter of ſuch importance ought, neverthelefs, to be difcuſſed, and agreed to
by you, in a General Aſſembly ; at which I
entreat you to affiſt by your Deputies, on
Sunday, the 8th of the enſuing month of
June, in the City of Corté. The Proviſional
Government will then ſuggeſt to you the
form and mode of the elections.

I be-

I befeech you to imprefs yourfelves with
the great importance of the affairs on which
you have to determine; and, on that account, let it be your care to felect perfons
of zeal, and acknowledged probity; and,
as much as may be in your power, repu-
table heads of families, interefted in good
Government and the profperity of the
Country. Let moderation and propriety of
conduct prevail in your Affemblies; that no
perfon among you may have the mortifi-
cation to remark any diforder in the moft
happy moment which has occurred in the
courfe of our revolutions, and in paffing
the moft important Act of Civil Society.
In the mean time, let every man fuggeft
whatever he may conceive moft ufeful
to the country, in order to communicate
his opinion to the Nation legally repre-
fented and affembled.

Corfica is now juftly regarded by Foreign
Powers as a Free Nation; her refolutions
will, I hope, be fuitable to her fituation,
and

and dictated by wifdom and by a love for
the publick good.

With refpect to myfelf, my dearly beloved Countrymen, after having devoted
every moment of my life to your happinefs,
I fhall efteem myfelf the happieft of man-
kind, if, through the means I have derived
from your confidence, I can obtain for our
Country the opportunity of forming a free
and lafting Government, and of preferving to Corfica it's name, it's unity, and it's
independence, whilft the names of the
Heroes, who have fpilt their blood in it's
fupport and defence will be, for future generations, objects of noble emulation and
grateful remembrance.

(Signed)   ·   PASQUALE DE PAOLI.

———————

Victory, Baftia Roads,
April 21, 1794.

S I R,
YOUR Excellency having been pleafed
to reprefent to us, on behalf of the Corfican

fican nation, that the intolerable and per-
fidious tyranny of the French Convention
having driven that brave people to take up
arms in their own defence, they were determined to fhake off altogether the unjuft
dominion of France, and to affert the right
of a Free and Independent Nation ; but being fenfible that their own efforts might be
infufficient to contend with France, or other
powerful nations, who might undertake
hoftile attempts againft them, and confiding
implicitly in the magnanimity and princely
virtues of His Britannick Majefty, and in
the bravery and generofity of his people,
they were defirous of forming a perpetual
Union with the Britifh Nation, under the
mild and equitable Government of his Majefty, and his Succeffors, for the better protection, and for the perpetual fecurity and
prefervation of their Independence and
Liberties: And your Excellency, having on
thefe confiderations, folicited, in the name
of the people of Corfica, His Majefty's
prefent affiftance, and His Royal protection
in time to come, we took the fame into our

moft

moſt ſerious conſideration ; and knowing
His Majeſty's gracious and affectionate diſ-
poſition towards the Corſican Nation, and
his readineſs to contribute in every way,
which is conſiſtent with juſtice and the in-
tereſts of his ſubjects, to the happineſs of
that brave people ; and being inveſted with
ſufficient power for that purpoſe, we determined to comply with your requeſt, and
have accordingly furniſhed the aid of His
Majeſty's Naval and Military Forces in the
Mediterranean, towards expelling the common enemy from the Iſland of Corſica.

We have ſince been honoured with more
ſpecial powers and authority to concert with
your Excellency and the people of Corſica ;
and finally to conclude on His Majeſty's
behalf, the particular form and mode of
relation which ſhall take placé between the
two Nations.

It is with the moſt lively ſatisfaction we
acquaint your Excellency, that we have it
in command from His Majeſty to aſſent, on
his

his part to fuch a fyftem as will cement the
Union of our two Nations under a common
Sovereign, and, at the fame time, fecure
for ever the independence of Corfica, and
the prefervation of her ancient Conftitution,
Laws, and Religion.

With whatever fatisfaction His Majefty
has gracioufly affented to propofitions,
which promife, perhaps, for the firft time,
not only to afford to this ifland the prefent
bleffings of tranquillity and peace, and a
fudden increafe of profperity and wealth,
but alfo to eftablifh it's national independence and happinefs, on a fecure and lafting
foundation, His Majefty is, however, determined to conclude nothing without the
general and free confent of the people of
Corfica.

We therefore requeft your Excellency
to take the proper fteps for fubmitting thefe
important matters to their judgment, and
as the fmall number of the enemy, at prefent invefted by the Britifh and Corfican

troops

troops, and which muſt ſoon either be de-
ſtroyed or yield to ſuperior force, can no
longer give any uneaſineſs to this country ;
but the freedom and deliverance of Corſica
is in effect accompliſhed, we beg leave to
ſubmit to your Excellency, whether it may
not be deſirable to take the earlieſt meaſures
for terminating theſe intereſting concerns,
and for adding a formal ſanction to that
Union which is already eſtabliſhed in the
hearts of all our countrymen.

We have the honour to be, &c.

(Signed)   Hood,
           Gilbert Elliot.
His-Excellency General Paoli.

TRANSLATION.

THE General Council charged with
the provincial Government of Corſica to
                         the

the Municipal Officers, Curates of Parifhes, and their Fellow-Countrymen.

Beloved Countrymen,

THE God of Armies, Protector of the moft Juft Caufe, has favoured your efforts.

The audacious army, whofe fury and violence was excited by the impious faction which propofed to itfelf to abolifh all order, cuftoms, and religion, in Europe, will fhortly be removed from our territories.

To fecure a more fpeedy fuccefs, Providence has given you the fupport of a powerful Nation, accuftomed to refpect laws, and a legitimate power, which has generoufly affifted you to extricate yourfelves from the tyrannical anarchy of the prefent Republic of France.

That Nation, and its King, offer you the advantages of a lafting Union and conftant protection.

F   The

The happy influence of our glorious
countryman, General de Paoli, added to
the refources of his genius, and excited by
the dangers of his own country, have acce-
lerated this happy event: In fhort, brave
Corficans, we are free.

By our conftancy, firmnefs, and courage,
we have acquired the enjoyment of the advantages we inherit from our Anceftors,
Liberty and Religion.

However, it would be but little to have re-
gained this noble fucceffion, if our efforts and
prudence were unable to fecure it for ever.

To infure the fuccefs of thofe efforts,
and to direct our prudence, a perfect Union
is neceffary ; our general refolutions muft
be formed with a view to our prefent fituation and our future expectations.

The Corficans muft therefore prefcribe
the form of Adminiftration and Government they chufe to adopt, enunciate, or
approve

approve of; and the principles on which it
is to be eftablifhed, or on which their Le-
giflation is to be fixed.

Finally, beloved Countrymen, the moft
important objeƈt is a fpeedy Union of the
people, and the laft Aƈt of the Provifional
Adminiftration you adopted, ordains us
to fupport the paternal and patriotic in-
tentions of General de Paoli.

In this invitation we can give you but a
faint idea of the important funƈtions you
will confide to your Reprefentatives in the
next Affembly; however, you no doubt
know the indifpenfible neceffity of adopting
meafures for the maintenance of internal
tranquillity, and of a form of Government
adapted to our cuftoms, powers, and fituation; and finally to the various relations
that will hereafter be eftablifhed between
Corficans: The Englifh Nation and their
King feel, even more than others, the neceffity that fuch Deputies fhould be appointed among our countrymen as fhall
have given evident proofs of their patriot-
ifm, and of their defire to aƈt with a zeal

adequate

adequate to the nature and importance of
their miffion, for eftablifhing and fecuring,
by the new order of things, not only for
the prefent, but in future, public felicity.
This laft confideration, in cafe you are fenfible of it, will, we are in hopes, determine you to prefer one of the moft refpectable heads of Family, in each of your
refpective communities, as a Reprefentative on fuch folemn and important occafions
in Council.

In this Union, which will form the moft
memorable crifis of our annals, the objects
muft be treated with that form and order
due to the dignity of the Reprefentatives of
a free people.

The ancient Affemblies of our Nation,
at the time of the glorious government of it's
deferving General, were only compofed of
one Deputy from each Community. Finding it neceffary to avoid the inconvenience
of repeated elections, we have thought it
expedient, in this circumftance, to invite
you to adopt this ancient cuftom ; chiefly on
reflecting

reflecting, that as harvest is approaching, the absence of Chiefs from their families, added to the expences of the journey and the time spent in the election, would be of prejudice to their affairs and domestic interests; the people will therefore establish constitutionally the number of it's Representatives for the successive Re-unions.

The zealous and good Citizens will, however, be enabled to lay before the Council their knowledge of all important subjects, which will be taken into consideration and discussed accordingly, but they will have no part in its deliberations.

The General Council therefore invites all Communities of Corsica to assemble on Sunday, the first of June; each to appoint, according to the form of election hereunto annexed, it's Representative at the General Council; and the General Assembly of the Clergy to take place on the Sunday following, the eighth of June.

The

The Municipal Officers, and parishes of the respective communities, are charged with the publication and distribution of both General Paoli's Circular, and this.

Corte, May 9, 1794.

For the General Council of the Government.

(Signed)

[A great number of Names.]

FORM OF ELECTION.

IN the year of 1794, on the 1st of June, in the Parish-Church of the Community of   , usual place for the General Meeting of the Clergy.

We N. N. N.* the Inhabitants of the said Community, exceeding the age of twenty-

* Here all names of such persons as shall be present at the Meeting will be affixed.

five,

five, being legally united by virtue of the circular letter wrote, on the 1ſt of May, by his Excellency General de Paoli, and the one wrote by the Provincial Government on the 9th of the ſame month, duly publiſhed, to appoint a Deputy, who is to be a Repreſentative at the General Council of Corſica, to be held on the 8th current; we have choſen as our Preſident Mr. N. „ the moſt proper perſon, among thoſe aſſembled, who knows how to write, and who has appointed as his Secretary Mr. N.

In ſucceſſion to the ſaid appointment, the majority of votes is given in favour of Mr. N. , father of a family, who has been duly elected by the preſent Aſſembly, and proclaimed Deputy; and unto him we give the power of concerting and treating, with the other Repreſentatives of the Nation, on the tranſactions that will in future take place between Corſica and His Majeſty the King of Great Britain, and the Engliſh Nation: as likewiſe on ſubjects of public utility, contained in the aforeſaid circular letter.

And

And the prefent verbal procefs has been regiftered and depofited in the Chancery of this Community ; and a copy given to ferve him, the faid Mr. N.   , Deputy, as a full power and certificate.

N. Prefident.
N. Secretary.

Firm of the General Council.

COTTONI, Vice Prefident.

MUSELLI, Secretary.

TRANSLATION.

WE the Reprefentatives of the Corfican Nation, free and independent, lawfully affembled in a General Meeting, poffeffed of a fpecial authority to form the prefent Conftitutional Act, have unanimoufly de‑ creed, under the aufpices of the Supreme Being, the following Articles :

C H A P.

CHAPTER I.

Of the Nature of the Conſtitution, and of the Conſtituted Powers.

ART. I. The Conſtitution of Corſica is Monarchical, according to the following fundamental laws.

ART. II. The Legiſlative Power is veſted in the King, and in the Repreſentatives of the People, lawfully elected and convened.

ART. III. The Legiſlature, compoſed of the King and of the Repreſentatives of the People, is denominated the Parliament; the Aſſembly of the Repreſentatives of the People is named the Houſe of Parliament; and the Repreſentatives are ſtiled Members of the Parliament.

CHAPTER II.

Of the Mode of Elections, the Number of Members, and the Functions of Parliament.

ART. I. The Territory shall be divided into pieves (districts) each of which shall send two Members to Parliament. The towns on the coast, of which the population shall amount to 3000 souls and upwards, have the right of sending two Members each to Parliament. The Bishops who discharge the duties of their See in Corsica, and are recognized as such by the Corsican Nation, shall be Members of Parliament.

ART. II. The Members of Parliament shall be elected by all the Corsican Citizens of twenty-five years of age, who shall have been resident at least one year in the pieve, or in the town, and who are possessors of land.

ART.

ART. III. No perfon fhall be elected a
Member of Parliament, unlefs he poffeffes at leaft 6060 livres in land in the
pieve, which he is to reprefent, and
and pays taxes in proportion to this poffeffion, and unlefs born of a Corfican
father, and bona fide an inhabitant, having kept houfe five years in the faid pieve,
and until he has arrived at the age of
twenty-five.

ART. IV. Lodgers, except thofe who are
inmates for life, perfons employed in
collecting the revenue, the receivers and
collectors of taxes, thofe who have pen-
fions, or who are in the fervice of a
foreign power, and priefts, cannot be
Members of the Houfe of Parliament.

ART. V. The form of election fhall be determined by the laws.

ART. VI. If a Member of the Parliament
dies, or becomes incapable, according to
law, of being a Member of Parliament,

3   another

another Member fhall be elected by his pieve, within fifteen days, by the King's authority.

ART. VII. The Houfe of Parliament has the right of enacting all the acts which are intended to have force of law.

ART. VIII. The Decrees of the Houfe of Parliament fhall not have force of law, unlefs they receive the King's fanction.

ART. IX. Any Decree that has not paffed the Houfe of Parliament, and received the King's fanction, fhall not be looked upon as law, nor carried into execution as fuch.

ART. X. No impofition, tax, or publick contribution fhall be laid without the confent of Parliament, or without being fpecially granted by it.

ART. XI. Parliament has the right of impeachment, in the name of the nation,

of

of every agent of government, guilty of prevarication, before the Extraordinary Tribunal.

ART. XII. The cafes of prevarication fhall be determined by the laws.

CHAPTER III.

Of the Duration and Convocation of Parliament.

ART. I. The duration of one Parliament fhall be two years.

ART. II. The King may diffolve the Parliament.

ART. III. In cafe of a diffolution of Parliament, the King fhall convene another within forty days.

ART. IV. Thofe perfons who were Members of the diffolved Parliament may be elected

elected Members of the succeeding one.

ART. V. If the Parliament expires without being diffolved, another fhall be called by the King's authority within forty days.

ART. VI. The King may prorogue the Parliament.

ART. VII. The Parliament cannot be convoked or affembled but by the King's command.

ART. VIII. The interval between the convening of the Houfe and it's prorogation; or if it be not prorogued until it's diffolution; or if it be not diffolved until it's expiration; is to be called the Seffion of Parliament.

ART. IX. The Vice-Roy, or, in cafe of illnefs, the Commiffioners nominated by him for that purpofe, fhall open the
Seffions

Seffions in perfon, and declare the reafons for convoking the Parliament.

ART. X. The Parliament may adjourn itfelf and re-affemble during the fame
Seffion.

ART. XI. The Houfe fhall decide upon
the contefted elections of it's Members.

ART. XII. The Members of Parliament
fhall not be fubject to arreft or imprifon-
ment for debt during the continuance of
their reprefentation.

CHAPTER IV.

*On the Mode or Deliberation, Freedom of De-
bate, and Internal Regulations of Parliament.*

ART. I. After the opening of Parliament
by the Vice-Roy, or by his Commiffioners, as is herein before mentioned,
the oldeft Member fhall take the Chair;
and

and the Members prefent having elected
a Provifional Secretary, amongft themfelves, fhall proceed to the choice of
a Prefident, and of one, or more Secretaries. The Secretaries fhall not be
chofen from among the Members, and
may be difmiffed by a vote of Parliament.

ART. II. The Parliament affembled, in all
the cafes before mentioned, has the power
of debate, and of paffing bills, whenever
above one half of it's Members are
prefent.

ART. III. Every Member elected, and not
appearing, fhall have notice from the
Prefident of the Houfe, to repair to his
poft within fifteen days.

ART. IV. In cafe of non appearance, or of
not fending a lawful excufe, fatisfactory
to the Houfe, fuch Member fhall be
condemned to a fine of 200 livres.

ART.

ART. V. Parliament may grant leave of absence, or permit the absence of such Members who solicit it, provided more than one half of it's Members remain present.

ART. VI. Every proposition made in Parliament shall be decided by the majority of the Members present; the President, in case of an equal division, shall give the casting vote.

ART. VII. The forms and procedures of enacting laws, and of determining other matters in the House, which may not be fixed by the present Constitution, shall be regulated by the House itself.

ART. VIII. The King's sanction, or the refusal of it, shall be announced in person, by the King's Representative in the House of Parliament, or by a special commission in case of sickness.

G   ART.

ART. IX. The form of the fanction shall be, The King approves; that of refusal, The King will examine; the bills fanctioned by the King are named, Acts of Parliament.

ART. X. No Member of Parliament shall be called to account, or punished by the King's fervants, for the opinions manifested, or the doctrines profeffed, in the Houfe, or by any other authority whatever, except by that of the Houfe itfelf.

ART. XI. The Prefident of the Parliament has the right of calling to order any of its Members when he may think proper. The Houfe may cenfure, arreft, and imprifon, any of its own Members during the feffion.

CHAPTER

CHAPTER V.

Upon the Exercife of the Executive Power.

ART. I. The King fhall have his immediate Reprefentative in Corfica, with the title of Vice-roy.

ART. II. The Vice-roy fhall have the power of giving his fanction or refufal to the decrees of Parliament.

ART. III. He fhall, moreover, have the power to perform, in the King's name, all the Acts of Government which are within the limits of the royal authority. There fhall be a Board of Council and a Secretary of State, nominated by the King; and mention fhall be made in the Vice-roy's orders, that he has taken the opinion of the faid Board of Council, and thefe orders fhall be counterfigned by the Secretary.

ART.

ART. IV. The nation has the right of peti-
tioning as well the Vice-roy as the Houfe
of Parliament. The conftituted and acknowledged corps of the law may petition
in a body, the other corps in their indi-
vidual capacity only; and a petition fhall
never be prefented by more than twenty
perfons, however numerous may be the
fignature to it.

ART. V. The Houfe of Parliament may
addrefs the King to recall his Vice-roy;
in fuch cafe the Houfe fhall addrefs His
Majefty in His Privy Council affembled :
The Vice-roy fhall be obliged to tranfmit
the addrefs to the King, upon the requifition of the Houfe, within the term of
fifteen days after fuch requifition; and
the Houfe may itfelf tranfmit it to the
King, even through the channel of a deputation : but, in any cafe, the Houfe
is bound to prefent to the Vice-roy,
fifteen days previous to the departure of
the addrefs, a copy of the fame, and of
the papers which are to accompany it.

ART.

ART. VI. The King has the exclufive direction of all military arrangements, and
is to provide for the internal and external
fecurity of the country.

ART. VII. The King declares war and
makes peace. He fhall not be authorifed,
however, in any event, nor on any account whatfoever, to give up, alienate, or
in any manner prejudice, the unity and
indivifibility of Corfica and its dependencies.

ART. VIII. The King fhall appoint to all
the offices of Government.

ART. IX. The ordinary employments of
juftice, and of the adminiftration of the
public money, fhall be conferred upon
natives of Corfica, or perfons naturalized
Corficans, in virtue of the laws.

G 3   CHAPTER

CHAPTER VI.

Of Judicial Proceedings, and of the Division of the Tribunals.

ART. I. Juſtice ſhall be executed in the King's name, and the orders carried into execution by officers appointed by him, in conformity to the laws.

ART. II. There ſhall be a Supreme Tribunal, compoſed of five Judges and the King's Advocate; and this ſhall be ſtationary in Corté.

ART. III. There ſhall be a Preſident and a King's Advocate attached to every other new juriſdiction.

ART. IV. The functions of the ſaid reſpective tribunals, their adminiſtration, and the emoluments, ſhall be determined by law.

ART.

ART. V. There shall be in every pieve a Podesta (Magistrate).

ART. VI. In every Community there shall be a Municipality, named by the people, and its functions shall be regulated by the laws.

ART. VII. Crimes, which deserve corporeal or ignominious punishments, shall be tried by the Judges and a Jury.

ART. VIII. The King has the power of granting pardon, in conformity to the same regulations under which he exercises this prerogative in England.

ART. IX. All civil, criminal, commercial causes, and those of every kind whatsoever, shall be terminated in Corsica, in the first and last instance.

CHAPTER

CHAPTER VII.

Of the Extraordinary Tribunal.

ART. I. There shall be an Extraordinary Tribunal, compofed of five Judges, appointed by the King, and commiffioned to judge upon any impeachment from the Houfe of Parliament, or upon all charges, made on the part of the King, of prevarication or other treafonable tranfactions.

ART. II. The nature of the faid crimes, and the form of trial, shall be determined upon by a fpecial law; but a Jury shall be allowed in every cafe of this fort.

ART. III. The Members of the Tribunal shall not affemble but in cafes of impeachment by the Houfe of Parliament, or by the King; and, immediately after judgment given, they shall be obliged to feparate.

CHAPTER

CHAPTER VIII.

Of Perfonal Liberty, and of the Liberty of the Prefs.

ART. I. No perfon fhall be deprived of his liberty and property but by fentence of the Tribunals acknowledged by the laws, and in the cafes and according to the forms prefcribed.

ART. II. Whoever fhall be arrefted, or placed in confinement, fhall be conducted, within the term of twenty-four hours, before the Competent Tribunal, in order that the caufe of his detention may be adjudged according to law.

ART. III. In cafe of the arreft being declared vexatious, the perfon arrefted will have a right of claiming damages and intereft before the Competent Tribunals.

ART.

ART. IV. The Liberty of the Prefs is de‑creed; but the abufe of it is to be amenable to the laws.

ART. V. Every Corfican fhall have the power freely to depart from his country, and to return to it with his property, con‑forming himfelf to the regulations and ordinances of General Police, obferved in fuch cafes.

CHAPTER IX.

Of the Corfican Flag and Navigation.

ART I. The ftandard fhall bear a Moor's head, quartered with the King's arms, ac‑cording to the form which fhall be pre‑fcribed by His Majefty.

ART. II. The King fhall afford the fame protection to the Trade and Navigation of the Corficans as to the Trade and Navigation of his other fubjects.

ART.

ART. III. The Corfican nation, deeply pe-
netrated with fentiments of gratitude towards the King of Great Britain and the
Englifh nation, for the munificence and
protection which it has always enjoyed,
and which is now, in a more fpecial
manner, fecured to it by the prefent Conftitutional Act,

Declares, That it will confider every attempt which in war, or in peace, fhall
be made to promote the glory of His
Majefty, and the Interefts of the empire
of Great Britain in general, as its own;
and the Parliament of Corfica will always
manifeft its readinefs and deference to
adopt all regulations, confiftent with its
prefent conftitution, which fhall be en-
acted by His Majefty in His Parliament
of Great Britain, for the extenfion and
advantage of the external commerce of
the empire and of its dependencies.

CHAPTER

CHAPTER X.

Of Religion.

ART. I. The Catholick, Apoftolick, Roman Religion, in all its evangelical purity, fhall be the only national religion in Corfica.

ART. II. The Houfe of Parliament is authorifed to determine on the number of Parifhes, to fettle the falaries of the Priefts, and to take meafures for enfuring the difcharge of epifcopal functions, in concert with the Holy See.

ART. III. All other modes of worfhip are tolerated.

CHAPTER XI.

Of the Crown and its Succeſſion.

The Sovereign King of Corfica is His Majefty George the Third, King of Great Britain,

Britain, and his fucceffors, according to the
order of fucceffion to the throne of Great
Britain.

CHAPTER XII.

*Of the Acceptance of the Crown, and of the
Conftitution of Corfica.*

ART. I. The prefent Act fhall be prefented
to His Majefty, the King of Great Britain, through His Excellency Sir Gilbert
Elliot, His Commiffary Plenipotentiary,
and fpecially authorifed for this purpofe.

ART. II. In the Act of Acceptance, His
Majefty, and His Plenipotentiary in His
name, fhall fwear to maintain the Liberty
of the Corfican Nation, according to the
Conftitution and the Laws; and the fame
oath fhall be adminiftered to His Succeffors, upon every fucceffion to the
throne.

ART.

ART. III. The Members of the Affembly
ſhall immediately take the following oath,
which ſhall be adminiſtered by His Excellency Sir Gilbert Elliot : " I ſwear
" for myſelf, and in the name of the
" Corſican Nation, which I repreſent,
" that I acknowledge for my Sovereign
" and King, His Majeſty George the
" Third, the King of Great Britain;
" to yield him faithful obedience, accord-
" ing to the Conſtitution and Laws of
" Corſica, and to defend the ſaid Conſti-
" tution and Laws."

ART. IV. Every Corſican ſhall, in his reſpective Community, take the preceding
oath.

Done, and unanimouſly decreed, and after
three readings, on three ſucceeding days, in
the General Affembly of the Corſican Nation,
in Corte this day, 19th June 1794, and individually ſigned in the affembly of all the
Members of which it is compoſed.

Signed by above four hundred names.

Con-

Continuation of the Seffions of the 19th *of June* 1794.

ALL the Members of the Affembly having individually figned the Conftitutional Act, it was propofed to prefent it to His Excellency Sir Gilbert Elliot, His Britannick Majefty's Commiffary Plenipotentiary, in order that it might be accepted by him in His faid Majefty's name. The Affembly having adopted this propofition, decreed, That the faid propofition fhall be made by a deputation of twelve Members, who were chofen and commiffioned for this purpofe.

After which, the Deputation having executed the commiffion affigned to them, re-entered the Hall, and with them the faid Sir Gilbert Elliot. The Members of the Affembly ftood up, during which he approached the Prefident, and pronounced the following acceptation :

I, the

I, the underfigned Baronet, Member of the Parliament of Great Britain, Member of the Privy Council, and Commiffary Plenipotentiary of His Britannick Majefty, having full power, and being fpecially authorized for this purpofe, do accept in the name of His Majefty George the Third, King of Great Britain, the Crown and Sovereignty of Corfica, according to the Conftitution, and to the Fundamental Laws contained in the Act of a General Affembly, held at Corte, and definitively fettled this fame day, the 19th of June, and as fuch offered to His Majefty; and, in His Majefty's name, I fwear to maintain the Liberty of the Corfican Nation, according to the Conftitution and to the Laws.

The prefent acceptation and oath is by us figned and fealed.

(L. S.)   Gilbert Elliot.

The faid acceptation and oath being read, the faid Sir Gilbert Elliot propofed to the Prefident, and to the Affembly, the Conftitutional

tutional Oath ; and this was taken by them in the following words :

" I fwear for myfelf, and in the name of
" the Corfican Nation, which I reprefent, to
" acknowledge for my Sovereign and King,
" His Majefty George the Third, the King
" of Great Britain, to yield him faithful
" obedience, according to the Conftitution
" and the Laws of Corfica, and to maintain
" the faid Conftitution and Laws."

The Conftitutional Act being entirely completed and finifhed, the Prefident adjourned the Seffion, and figned the above, as did alfo the Secretaries, the year, month, and day abovementioned.

(Signed)
    PASQUALE DE PAOLI, Prefident.
    CARLO ANDREA POZZO DI BARGO,
       Secretary.
    GIO ANDREA MUSELLI, Secretary.

H   TRANS-

˙ TRANSLATION.

*Speech made in the General Assembly of Corsica
on the Acceptation of the Crown and Constitution of that Island, by His Excellency
Sir Gilbert Elliot.*

Gentlemen,

IN availing myself, for the first time, in
the midst of the Corsican Nation, of the privilege of calling you Brothers and Fellow-
Citizens; a reflection, which will naturally
occur to every one, excites in me the most
heart-felt satisfaction. Independent of the
reciprocal political advantages which we may
derive from so close a connection, I see, on
the present occasion, every thing that can
render it more precious and more estimable
by the sentiments of confidence and of affec-
tion, the first and pure principles of our
union, which they will ever continue to
cement and consolidate.

This

This remarkable truth, which it is impoffible to overlook, cannot be mentioned without a ftrong emotion of fenfibility and joy. Our two Nations have, for a long period, been diftinguifhed by a reciprocal and remarkable efteem. Without anticipating the happy end to which this inftinctive partiality, this fympathetic attraction, may fome day lead us, we have given to each other inftances of confidence on every occafion; yet no relations have hitherto fubfifted between us, except thofe of reciprocal and voluntary good offices. Our minds have been prepared by Providence for the fate which awaited us; and the Divine Goodnefs, intending our union, has ordained that it fhould be anticipated and brought about (if I may fo exprefs myfelf), by a fimilarity of character, and by a conformity of views and principle, and, above all, by a pleafing exchange of friendly fervices.

This facred compact, which I received from your hands, is not a cold and interefted

H 2   agreement

agreement between two parties who meet
by accident, and form a contract founded on
the impulse of the moment, or on a selfish
and temporary policy—No; the event of this
happy day is only the completion of wishes
we had previously formed; to-day our hands
are joined, but our hearts have been long
united, and our motto should be, *Amici &*
non diventura.

However seducing this prospect of our
happiness may appear, I trust (and it is important for us to know it, as we assuredly do)
that it does not depend on sentiment alone;
but that it rests on the solid basis of the true
interests and permanent felicity of the two
Nations.

I will not mention to you the interests of
Great Britain upon this occasion; not that
they are of little consequence, but being of a
nature purely political, the subject would be
too cold, too dry, for this important day.
Besides, it is not necessary, on this occasion,
to appreciate them in detail. I shall confine

4 myself

myfelf to this remark, that every poffible advantage which Great Britain could have in
view from her union with Corfica, is effen-
tially attached to your political and abfolute
independence of every European Power;
and that thefe advantages are not only com-
patible with your interefts, but cannot for
the moft part exift, and ftill lefs flourifh, but
in proportion to your profperity. .

On your part, what is neceffary to render
you a happy people? I will tell you in
two words, Liberty at home and fecurity
abroad.

Your Liberty will not be expofed to any
encroachments from a Monarch, who, by
his own experience, and the example of his
anceftors for feveral generations, is perfuaded
that the liberty and the profperity of his
people is the only foundation of the power,
the glory, and the fplendour of the throne.
A King who has ever governed according
to the laws, and whofe fceptre is at once
ftrengthened by the privileges, and embel-

H 3   lifhed

lifhed by the happinefs of his fubjeds.
Here I might expatiate on the auguft virtues of that Monarch whom you have chofen
for your own; but they are known to all
his fubjeds: You will therefore become ac-
quainted with them by a happy and certain
experience, and this teftimony will be far
more faithful than my weak voice.

It would not, however, be right, that your
Liberty fhould depend folely on the perfonal
virtues of the Monarch. You have therefore been careful to enfure it by the wife
Conftitution and fundamental Laws of our
Union, which, in my opinion, conftitute fo
effential a part of the Act you prefent to me
this day, that I could not (without violating
the confidence repofed in me by my Sovereign) agree to a fyftem which might
have degenerated into tyranny; a condition
equally unfavourable to the happinefs of him
who exercifes it, and of thofe who endure it.

If His Majefty therefore accepts the
Crown, which you have agreed to offer him,
it

it is becaufe he is determined to protect, and never to enflave thofe from whom he receives it; and, above all, becaufe it is given, and not feized upon by violence.

For external fecurity, you wanted nothing but the conftant and active alliance of a maritime power. This act enfures it to you; and whilft you enjoy at home peace and tranquillity, which the enemy will no longer be able to interrupt, you will fhare with us the treafures of trade and the fovereignty of the feas.

From this day therefore you are quiet and free. To preferve thefe bleffings, you have only to preferve your ancient virtues, courage, and the facred love of your country. Thefe are the native virtues of your foil; they will be enriched by thofe which accompany our union, and which you will derive from our induftry, from our long experience (that true fource of political wifdom), and from our love of Liberty, at once enthufiaftic and enlightened. I fpeak of

H 4   that

that Liberty which has for its object to
maintain your civil rights and the happiness
of the people ; not to ferve ambition and
vice : That Liberty which is infeparable
from religion, order, refpect for the laws,
and a facred regard for property, the firft
principles of every human fociety ; that
Liberty which abhors every kind of defpotifm, and efpecially that moft terrible of all
defpotifm which arifes from the unreftrained
violence of the human paffions. Such are
the virtues which belong both to you and to
us ; on their happy mixture and influence on
each other depends the profperity of Corfica.
Immediate Liberty, and a progreffive and
increafing profperity. Such is the text ;
to which I hope and venture to predict, that
our behaviour to each other, and our common deftinies, will always prove a faithful
and a fatisfactory illuftration.

Number of the Jurifdictions, Fiefs, Villages, Families,
and Inhabitants, in the whole Ifland of Corfica.

	Vil.	Fam.	Inh.
Capo Corfo,	10	1480	6410
Fief of Brando,	5	538	2386
Fief of Caneri,	1	145	618
Fief of Nonza,	4	227	962
Jurifdiction			
Of Baftia,	95	6473	28841
Of Nebio,	14	1177	5148
Of Aleria,	34	2003	9087
Of Corte,	71	3328	14766
Of Calvi,	7	998	4421
Of Balagna,	30	2134	9489
Of Ajaccio,	83	4650	21246
Of La Rocca, or Sartene,	27	1451	6647
Of Portovecchio and Bonifacio,	2	570	2500
Of Vico,	33	1033	4888
Of the Fief d'Iftria,	11	650	2980
Total,	**427**	**26854**	**120389**

APPENDIX.

―――――――――

MEMORIAL,

PRESENTED TO THE

NATIONAL ASSEMBLY,

Concerning the Exploitation of the WOODS, *or felling of the* TIMBER, *in* CORSICA.

THE INTRODUCTION.

A GREAT Economy in the expenditure of the ſtate being one of the principal means whereby the National Aſſembly will be enabled to lighten the public burdens; any plan tending thereto cannot fail of being favourably received.

The propoſed alleviation does not conſiſt in the ſuppreſſion of uſeful employments

or

or neceffary expences, but on the contrary (without requiring any previous aid from the public Treafury) procures new advantages to a confiderable portion of the French nation.

The twofold advantages refulting from this propofal muft neceffarily entitle the projector to countenance and encouragement. The author has only to regret that what he propofes having equally in view the benefit of the ftate and that of private individuals, fhould be confined to a fingle province, viz. the Ifland of Corfica.

This ifland, the acquifition of which coft forty millions of livres, has been thefe twenty years in the poffeffion of France. Since that period it has annually ftood us in nine hundred thoufand livres.—Thus, fo far from contributing in the leaft to the maintenance of the ftate, Corfica has not even been productive of a revenue equal to the expence it has occafioned.

Independent

Independent of the fum of fix hundred
thoufand livres, raifed annually in this
country by direct and indirect impofts,
Adminiftration has been under the neceffity
of remitting annually nine hundred thoufand livres from France; whereof three
hundred thoufand were fet apart to defray
the civil expences; and the remaining fix
hundred thoufand were deftined for the
payment of the extra troops kept up in the
ifland for the fafety of this part of the
empire.

It is poffible, that a reduction may be
hereafter effected in the general expenditure
relative to Corfica, in confequence of the
new fyftem of Adminiftration which is
fhortly to be introduced in the feveral parts
of the French empire, to which the inhabitants have fo folemnly acceded. But it is
a matter of doubt, whether the trivial impofts, which this Province feems at prefent
to bear with fuch difficulty, will be ever
adequate to the defraying of it's provincial
expences, even fuppofing a confiderable reduction

duction fhould take place in the civil and more efpecially the military eftablifhments.

Regiments are more expenfive in this Province than in any other part of the empire. Our forces cannot, however, be withdrawn, fhould even the inhabitants, who certainly are very brave, take upon themfelves the defence of the ifland. The country would be expofed to a great fcarcity of fpecie, and be deprived of the fole means, in the actual ftate of things, of difpofing to advantage of thofe provifions which their feeble population cannot confume.

Thus, unlefs a new field be opened for exertion of induftry in Corfica, the ifland fo far from having the means of contributing to the fupport of the public revenue, muft neceffarily remain burthenfome to the ftate.

It is, therefore, important for the nation to favour and encourage every induftrious effort in this Province, and to enable it
thereby

thereby to contribute one day to the general receipts of the empire.

One of the greatest refources of Corfica confifts in it's extenfive woods; and it will be proved hereafter, that, on applying the produce of induftry to this article, there may, in a fhort time, be raifed a fufficient fum to defray the annual expences of the country, which having once attained this firft degree of profperity, could not fail, under the aufpices of liberty, of making a progreffional improvement in every refpect.

SECTION I.

Art. I. Extent of Corfica, and it's Woods.

The fuperficies of Corfica from the moft exact meafurement and ftatement, copied from the Roll Books, upon a fcale of one line to five and twenty *Toifes*, which makes the nine-tenths of the extent of the ifland, being five hundred and forty fquare leagues: it's length, in toifes, is two thoufand two hundred and eighty-two. Corfica, there-

fore

fore, contains two millions eight hundred thoufand acres. Confidering the nature of the foil, this fuperficies is divided into feven twentieths, or thereabouts, containing nine hundred and eighty thoufand acres of barren and inacceffible rocks covered here and there with a few larch trees of little value: eight twentieths, or one million one hundred and twenty thoufand acres of uncultivated and open land fit for planting wood, bearing at prefent nothing but infignificant fhrubs; two twentieths, or two hundred and eighty thoufand acres of various culture; and three twentieths, or four hundred and twenty thoufand acres of foret woods, and lofty trees, called *Makis,** which are nearly equal to a coppice in France of twenty years growth.

Art. II. Different Sorts of Wood.

The foreft trees, termed *Futaies,* being more than one half of the whole, confift,

* The *Makis* confift in fmall oak-holm, arbutus, turpentine, and juniper trees; yew, myrtle, box of the greater kind; in olive and wild fruit trees.

according

according to fituation, of noble pines, firs, and other various coniferous trees, oak-holm, cork, beach, afh, and chefnut.

The proprietors of woods know, by con-ftant experience, that a common coppice of thirty years ftanding will give twenty cords per acre: the cord is eight foot long (King's meafure) by four in height and three and a half in depth; the whole forming a hundred and twelve cubic feet in apparent bulk; fixty fix folid cubic feet, and weighing nearly forty quintals.

It is equally clear, by common experience, ιat one acre of foreft trees, inftead of giving thirty cords will yield thirty fix, in propor-tion as thefe trees double the term of their growing; that is to fay, trees of fixty or eighty years ftanding will produce more in proportion than thofe of only twenty years growth. If fuffered to remain ftanding beyond eighty years, foreft trees will yield timber of double the value of cord wood, deftined only for firing.

I

Art,

Art. 3. This Produce calculated in Cords.

The extent of the foreft trees, and that of the larger *Makis* are, in Corfica, of a quantity nearly equal : thefe Makis give thirty cords per acre. The former fuppofing them to be of only fixty years ftanding, give about a hundred cords; the medium is fixty five cords, by which multiplying the 420,000 acres of wood of all kinds in this ifland; the refult of the operation will be twenty feven million three hundred thoufand cords of wood deftined for fuel.

Art. IV. Quantity proportioned to the Population of the Ifland.

Before we examine the feveral ufes the woods in Corfica are moft fit for, it would be proper to anticipate an objection that might be made, on the fuppofition that too great a fall of thefe extenfive woods would deprive the ifland of one of it's moft neceffary articles of life. My anfwer is that the real quantity of this produce may be eafily afcertained,

certained, as the originals of the accurate
typographical ſtatements are depoſited at
the War Office.—This objection, therefore,
falls immediately to the ground. In fine, an
eſtimate might be made by ſimple analogy,
that there is in Corſica a vaſt quantity of
wood and far exceeding it's conſumption.
In fact, wood is a general and ſpontaneous
production of nature ; it covers every part
of the earth, and man, conſidering the limited ſtate of population, cannot equally
cultivate or apply it to the moſt uſeful
purpoſes. Thus wood is every where
found in proportion to the extent of land,
and ever proves the inverſe of it's population.

Now in France, where there are twenty
four millions of inhabitants upon a ſurface
of twenty ſeven thouſand ſquare leagues,
or a hundred and thirty five million acres,
which makes nearly five acres and a half
per head, wood cannot be ſaid to be ſcarce,
though every ſpecies of induſtry in which
firing is principally inſtrumental has been

I 2 exerciſed

exercifed for ages paft. In Corfica, on the contrary, where for time immemorial little or no encouragement has been given to manufactories, the number of inhabitants fcarce amounts to one hundred and fifty thoufand, upon a furface of two million eight hundred thoufand acres, which bears the proportion of eighteen acres and two thirds per man. There muft, therefore, be a very confiderable increafe of population and a great fpur given to induftry, before the Corficans can have any real want of one fourth of the wood the ifland contains.

Yet as a due allowance fhould be made, in proportion to the actual ftate of the population of the country, it would be proper to let our calculation be formed on a broad fcale.

Marfeilles is fuppofed to contain more than two thirds of the population of all Corfica. They import here their timber from the Coaft of Frejus, St. Topes,

I   from

from the iflands of Corfica and St. Peter,
from Sardinia, Dauphiné, Burgundy,
and from the northern parts of Europe.
On examining the Entry Books and com-
paring the Regifter of two fucceffive
years, it will be found that the annual im-
ports of this place does not exceed four
hundred thoufand weight of wood of different forts, which makes four quintals,
table weight, or three quintals and a quarter
Avoirdupois, equivalent to forty thoufand
cords. Therefore the confumption of Corfica eftimated at fixty thoufand cords would
undoubtedly be overated, it having neither
fhip building nor manufactories in the
ifland; it's confumption, being thus confined to the article of common firing, could
by no means equal that of a fingle city
bafking in the fun-fhine of opulence, and
enjoying the fulleft extent of profperity.

In order to enable Adminiftration to afcertain the local confumption of wood in
Corfica, during the fpace of forty years, a
referve need only be made of about forty

thoufand

thoufand acres, equal to two million four
hundred thoufand cords, which deduɔted
from twenty feven million three hundred
thoufand (the fuppofed growth of the country) leave a remainder of five and twenty
million of cords applicable to the ufe we are
going to indicate,

Art. V. Exaɔt Eftimate of the total Value
of thefe Woods.

To excite in the public a defire of employing to the greateft advantage thefe extenfive woods, which have for ages fprung
up, attained their maturity, and decayed,
without being exploited, therefore without
producing the leaft benefit to man, we have
only to appreciate it's worth : In order not
to be deceived in our calculation, we muft
view it in it's moft difadvantageous light,
which is that of reducing it to charcoal.
Now the price of this commodity, in every
acceffible part of France, runs from ten fols
the quintal to fifty : So that the medium
price will be, at leaft, thirty fols per quintal,

A cord

A cord of wood weighing more than forty quintals, and the charcoal weighing one fourth of the wood in it's original ftate:* The cord of wood produces ten quintals of charcoal, and twenty five millions of cords give two hundred and fifty thoufand millions of quintals. Which at the medium of thirty fols is worth three hundred and fixty five million of French livres.

It may be objected that the coal is not ready made and is confequently attended with previous expence; in reply to this obfervation, I anfwer, that it's preparation requiring no capital, and refulting from the moft ruftic induftry, *is a material acquifition to Society*, by furnifhing employment to a great number of it's members, who would otherwife be at a lofs for occupation, and become more or lefs buthenfome to the ftate.

* Du Hamel.Art. du Charbonier.

I 4 *Art.*

Art. VI. Industry triples the Value.

Moreover this combuftible, called charcoal, whenever it can (as is the cafe in Corfica) be advantageoufly employed in the
metallurgical arts, is to be confidered as a
mere inftrument of art, and the inftrument
which ferves to the exercife of any art
whatever, being only a part of the value
of what it helps to produce; it follows,
with due regard to the value of wood, coal,
and iron taken collectively, that the two
hundred and fifty millions of quintals, worth
three hundred and feventy five millions,
which Corfica can furnifh with eafe, and
applicable to Metallurgical purpofes (of
which this combuftible is the main and moft
indifpenfible material) may prove the means
of an induftrious occupation of quadruple
value. It will appear in the fequel, that
the full amount thereof is, on a fair efti-
mation, not overated at twelve hundred
millions, divided by the number of years
which

which ferve to regulate the feveral
terms of cutting the faid woods. In the
mean time the wood, felled in regular
progreffion, having been cleared away, the
premifes would be renewing, and in due
time would afford new materials for frefh
enterprifes in future, and fo on *ad infini-
tum.*

Art. VII. *Divifion of a general Exploitation to be effected in forty years.*

It is thought that the woods in Corfica
do not become fit for ufe under a growth of
forty years; dividing the totality, therefore, by this term, we fhall be able to
afcertain the amount of the annual fall of
timber, &c. throughout the ifland; and although, we have already fhewn, that a referve of forty thoufand acres fhould be
made for the occafional exigencies of the
inhabitants of the ifland; forty thoufand
more acres, or the tenth part of the woods
might be left ftanding eighty years, and the
immediate

immediate demands for prefent confumption might be taken out of the three hundred and eighty thoufand acres, marked out for the ax, and deftined to be cleared away every fortieth year.

Art. VIII. Different ufes to be made of the feveral forts of Wood in Corfica.

The moft advantageous ufe that the woods in Corfica can be put to is as follows :—

The *Makis*, a dwarf fpecies of tree from fix inches to two feet round, very feldom exceeds from ten to twenty feet in height (French meafure) ; and is only fit for charcoal and fire wood.

The *Oak-holm*, which is the moft abundant of any, is from three to nine feet thick, by twenty to fifty feet high. The body when found will furnifh houfe timber, ribs, and forky pieces of wood for the building of

merchant

merchant ſhips, ſuch as *varangues*, *fourcats*, allonges de revers, pieces d'etrave, &c.*
The branches and hollow trunks will ſell for fuel, or may be converted into charcoal.

Pines, from three feet round (if leſs in dimenſion they ſhould by no means be cut down) to twelve by forty, to eighty feet high, would ſerve for large *maſting*, *yardarms*, and *beams*, of a larger ſize, *ſide planks*,

* Inſtead of exporting wood in it's own natural ſtate to Provence, where it ſells but for fifty ſols, there is a far more advantageous mode of diſpoſing of the ſame, which is by employing it in the country for ſhip building, &c. as it may be beſt to turn to account. Oak-holms, in Corſica, whether ſtrait, crooked, or forked, ſerve conjointly for membranes, &c. The pine will furniſh the *bordages*, or ſide planks, the *pont*, or decking, the *antennes*, or ſail yards, maſts, &c. The hard yew, box, and olive trees ſerve for the making of pullies. Wood thus employed, inſtead of requiring a number of bottoms for it's conveyance to a foreign market, would itſelf be uſefully employed in exporting abroad the different productions of the iſland. Other materials, ſuch as iron work for the rudder, pegs, pins, &c. together with tar, for the *calfatage*, or calking (the ſtaying of the ſeams) they are to be had on the ſpot. So that nothing is wanted from abroad, to fit out a veſſel compleat, but ſails and rigging.

and

and *madriers*, a fort of plank exceeding two inches in thicknefs, rafters, common boards and *voliges*, a thin kind of plank ufed in the roofing of houfes.

Thofe trees, which are damaged * may be converted into charcoal, as likewife thofe that are *couronnès* (grubby and ftumpy) and *champignonnèes* (*wrankled*) the charcoal made from thefe trees, if intermixed with that of the oak-holm, may be of infinite ufe, in the manner I am going to fhew.

SECTION II.

Art. I. Iron Forges.

The beft and moft profitable way of employing wood in Corfica would be the fupplying the forges with fuel. What is felled and hewn into timber, being fold by the cubic foot is not more productive, in point of gain, than what is reduced on the fpot to charcoal and confumed in the forges.

* The country people apply fire to the roots, in order to fet the turpentine a running.

This

This object, indeed, is of a very limited extent. In fine, what is exported to Provence for firing, though it fells well and yields a profit of thirty per cent. would turn to a better account in furnishing fuel for the domestic forges. Therefore, it is obvious, that this is the main object, and consequently that which ought defervedly to have the preference.

Art. II. The Catalonian Forges.

The most ferviceable forge in Corfica is that species which is generally ufed in the ifland, greatly refembling the Catalonian forge. It differs from the high forges ufed in France, for working mineral fubftance of an inferoir quality, and which they are obliged to run into pigs, as in Burgundy, Berry, Nivernois, Franche Comté, Lorraine, Champagne, and Normandy, where the mines are commonly of a fandy and gravelly nature, yielding no more than fifteen or twenty pounds of forged iron to the quintal.

Art.

Art. III. Comparison between the Catalonian Forges and the High Furnaces.

The erecting the high furnaces and other adjacent buildings generally cost eighty thousand livres. The quantity of forged iron which they are enabled to produce is thirty quintals per day; but from a variety of accidents they are liable to, these furnaces are subject to frequent interruption during the year.

Two Catalonian forges yielding nearly the same quantity of forged iron per day, cost at most from ten to twelve thousand livres; if built on the best construction will be less exposed to the inconvenience of occasional interruption.

By the process of high furnaces, each pound of forged iron requires six or seven pounds of coal. According to the Catalonian process carried to the highest perfection in Roussillon, and Foix, three pounds only, or at most three pounds and a half are con-

5   sumed

fumed in producing one pound of faleable iron. Thus there is a manifeft economy in the article of fuel, being one half leis; befides a confiderable reduction of more than five fixths in the primary expences in forming the eftablifhment.

Thefe forges have another advantage; which is, that without any extraordinary procefs, a part of the iron therein worked, that is to fay the furface of the *Maffets*, or lumps, is fpontaneoufly converted into native fteel, or ftrong iron, double in value to the interior part which is of a fofter quality, and which is generally a twentieth or a twenty fifth part of the whole.

This procefs, however, is only applicable to flinty mineral, that abounds in metal. Experiments have been made in Foix with the *Berry Mineral*, but without fuccefs *. Corfica, though not in the actual poffeffion

* Thefe experiments have been very carefully made, under the infpection of the Baron de Dietrich, Member of the Academy of Sciences, at the Marquis de Gudane's forges,

poffeffion of this production, within it's own territory, has the advantage of being able to procure, on eafy terms, from the ifland of Elbe, a kind of mineral, which is fitter than any to be worked according to the procefs of the Catalonian forges.

Art. IV. The Iron Mine of the Ifland of Elbe.

This mine is within fight of Corfica, and at fifteen leagues diftance: It is one of the moft confiderable *Depôt* of exterior metallics in the known* world. All naturalifts agree, that it will laft for ages; and Pliny afferts, that the general foil of the ifland has a metallic tendency: in this opinion, he is backed by the general obfervations of antiquity. The rocky mineral, which

forges, in the Province of Foix, by Mr. Vergnies de Eouifchere, the moft ingenious proprietor of forges in that Canton, where iron works are brought to fuch perfeftion.

" * It has been obferved on the approach of a fhip, " that the magnetic virtue of thi* mineral is fo great that " it deranges the compafs."

which it produces, is one of the richeft in Europe, as it frequently gives feventy five pounds of pure metal per quintal, and never lefs than fifty. Another excellent quality, in it's nature, is that it's metal is lefs affected by the mixture and adhefion of heterogeneous fubftance : befides it is of eafy fufion, and contains abundance of *unincorporated fulphur*, a fmall quantity of *fulphur of iron*, of *filice* (a flinty fubftance) and of *oxigene* (vital air): Sometimes it becomes a pure *oxide* of iron ; which fignifies the combining of the principle of the acid with iron. It's price, at the fea fide, is twenty four fols per *cantaro*, containing one hundred and fifty pounds Genoefe weight, or one quintal avoirdupois French weight.

This mineral fubftance is, of all others, perhaps, the beft adapted to the procefs of the Catalonian forges : for, according to a long ftanding practice in Corfica, which, though fingular of itfelf, has a great analogy thereto, the quantity of iron here worked is but very inconfiderable, for they ufe only

K   charcoal

charcoal made of the chefnut, when dead, which confines and retards the fabrication; thefe trees being to be met with on the Eaftern coaft alone of the ifland, and the fruit ferving in lieu of bread, the natives are naturally defirous of preferving an article fo neceffary as long as poffible; they are, therefore, left growing till they decay. This accounts for the reluctance with which the chefnut tree is, in Corfica, refigned by the inhabitants to the devouring flames of a furnace.

Art. V. Procefs followed in Corfica in the management of the Iron Ore, of the Ifland of Elbe.

The mode of treating this mineral is as follows:—A femi-elliptic pyramid is erected with pieces of charcoal, five inches long, upon a flat area, this pile is twenty feet by ten wide, and eighteen inches high, and is placed before the wall, that inclofes the funnel, through which the wind is conveyed by a fingle tube, called *Trompe,* from fifteen

to

to twenty feet of perpendicular height. Outfide of this pile is placed the previoufly roafted ore, which is deftined for immediate fufion; thick lumps of raw mineral, intended for the fubfequent melting, furrounds the whole and receives a firft roafting. The infide of the pyramid is filled with other coal, which is the fuel that is to communicate heat to the whole work. This again is covered with a ftrong layer of coal duft and cinders, in order to prevent the external air from penetrating.

In a fpace of three hours the broken pieces of ore, which touches outwardly the half round of charcoal, and acting in fome meafure as a crucible, will be found to have received a laft and more thorough baking than the previous one. The faid ore glutinates into cakes, and the vitrifying part thereof will then be in the *firft ftate of fufion* (en laitier.)

This operation being finifhed, the pyramid is then demolifhed and replaced by two

freſh

fresh heaps of cinders on the right and left of the pipe, which is, as it were, buried under the coal that fills this space. Opposite to the pipe, and as near as possible to it, the mineral cakes are now successively placed upon the coals. A fourth of these cakes produce, in four hour's time, a forgeable *masselet*, or lump of iron. This process continues till all the caked mineral has undergone the violent action of an intense heat, which serves to clear it of all heterogeneous matter; this operation lasts for about twenty hours. Thus we see the whole process of a melting, in Corsica, which is performed in four and twenty hours: but it produces no more than two quintals and a half of saleable, or marketable, iron, or three at most, consuming about five quintals of raw mineral, and nine or ten quintals of charcoal.

Art. VI. Description of the Catalonian Forge.

This species of forge consists in an open room, forty feet square, under which a furnace, or crucible, is placed, of about

two

two feet fquare, raifed a foot from the ground, and fixed to one of the thick walls of the inclofure. A large hammer, of twelve or fifteen hundred weight, occupies one fide of the fquare, it is put in motion by an apparatus fimilar to that ufed in the refining works, and *renardieres* of the high forges. The anvil, which is even with the ground, and called the *ftock*, is fupported by a hard and large ftone block, or by a col-lection of maffy *parallepipeds* of iron joined perpendicularly, and clofed in by an under ground brick-work. Acrofs the wall, that forms one fide of the crucible, the pipe paffes pointing downwards, and fupplies the air introduced into the wind cafe by one or two pipes, which in thefe forges are ufed in lieu of bellows, being far more econo-mical, as they do not coft one eighth of a pair of bellows, eight of which are requifite in the forges of high furnaces, in the re-finery and heating houfes,

These forges are ferved by eight work-men, viz. a *foyer*, a *maillet*, two *efcolas*,

two

two *piquemines,* and two *fervans.* their
pay is rated by the quantity of iron
they forge or caft, fo that the price of the
fabrication never exceeds forty fols the
quintal ; and the workmen's wages are from
twenty to three livres, or forty fols, one day
with another.

Art. VII. Procefs or Operation.

Inftead of running the ore into pigs and
then melting it, till it drops fit for refinement,
the procefs of thefe Catalonian forges confifts
in filling the fection of the crucible, on the
fide of the wind-pipe, with charcoal, which
fmothers the tube as it were ; the oppofite
fide of the crucible is then filled up with
ore, previoufly roafted and broken up to the
fize of a nut. The fire is lighted up, the pipe
is filled with wind, and, from time to time,
the *laitier* formed from the vitrious part of
the ore is fet a running, which is done by
paffing through a hole, called the *chio,* a
ringard which penetrates into the baking
fubftance. In three hours the iron forms
itfelf

5

itself into a *maſſet* or *loupe* (heap) at the bottom of the crucible. This maſs, or heap, is then taken out and divided into two or four *maſſelottes*, or parcels, which are heated anew, and formed into bars by means of the great hammer ; the whole operation is accompliſhed in ſix hours time.

Art. VIII. *Productions from Iron.*

Theſe forges are able, every four and twenty hours, to furniſh four parcels of four quintals each ; but as they are liable to frequent interruption, through occaſional accidents, ſuch as the breaking of the ſtone bottom of the furnace, or the neceſſary repairs of the crucible, theſe forges are ſuppoſed to produce two quintals per day, which is ſeventy-two quintals per week, and about three thouſand ſix hundred quintals per annum.

Art. IX. *The Trompes, or Water Conduits.*

Theſe water conduits, ſupplying the place of bellows, require a fall of water which,

however,

however, is eafily to be procured by means
of a dyke on a rivulet, fufficient to furnifh
a body of water of eight or nine fectional
inches fquare. Thefe conduits are much
ufed in mountainous countries, fuch as
Dauphiné, Rouffillon, Spanifh Navarre,
Tirol, the Apennines and Corfica.

Art. X. Of Charcoal and Native Steel.

The proper fuel for the Catalonian
forges is the charcoal made of the following
wood: The oak-holm, cork, larch, pine,
arbutus, privet, beach and turpentine trees.
Thefe may be ufed feparately or intermixed,
according to the effect each of them apart
might produce, or on mixing; in fine,
according to the quality required in the fteel,
whether foft or hard. Certain it is, that the
coals made of light and foft wood render
the iron foft, for which reafon they are
termed *foft coal*; whereas the coal formed
of heavy and hard wood (as the oak-holm,
which weighs about ninety pounds per
cubic foot) is better calculated for producing
native

native fteel, or hard iron, which is fometimes faulty in producing what is called *rou-
verains*, (brittle) when not attended to with
the greateft care. But the blending thefe
different coals produces iron of the beft
quality, viz. that which unites the greateft
tenacity to the moft perfect ductility, or
malleability; and you may acquire either
of thefe qualities in a greater or leffer degree, in proportion as the procefs is carried
on with greater or lefs activity. A flow fire
of foft coal produces foft iron ; on the contrary, a very fharp inceffant fire of hard
coal contributes much to the formation of
ftrong tough iron, or natural fteel*.

SECTION

* Some feem to think, that fince they ufe the chefnut
wood coal in the fabrication of the iron ore brought from
the ifland of Elbe, and principally the coal made of the dry
or dead chefnut tree, or fome other light wood ; that the
oak-holm or cork tree coal would by no means be proper
for fimilar operations. It has been obferved, that hard
wood naturally renders the iron brittle, and it is fuppofed
this charcoal contains a *phofphoric acid*, which commu-
nicates *phofphorus* to the coal itfelf in the act of burning,
when it coalefces with the *carbone*, or the coal, di-
vefted of it's acid; that when the charcoal is applied

to

SECTION III.

Art, I. *The Quantity of Wood that will serve*
for Timber, and Planks.

We have already obferved, that of the
four hundred and twenty thoufand acres of
wood

to a mineral body the *phofphorus* therein contained, forms
in the metal *phofphate* of iron, or what is called *fyderite,*
which renders it brittle; but it appears, on the contrary,
on a thorough inveftigation of the matter by Meffrs.
Vandermonde, Bertholet, and Monge, that it is not in
this manner the feveral forts of charcoal operate upon iron,
in the fabrication of which they are ufed. In a very interefting Memorial inferted in the Hiftorical Accounts of
the Academy of Sciences for the year 1786, thefe learned
men gave it as their opinion, " that charcoal, in it's natural
ftate, blends with the iron in the feveral ftages of the procefs, and that it is which chiefly tends to give a particular
quality to the mineral in it's ftate of fufion; hence chymifts
fay, *fontes blanches* (a white caft), *fontes grifes* (grey caft),
fer forgé dur (hard caft iron), *l'acier malléable* (malleable
fteel), *acier intraitable* (ftubborn fteel). In fine, that the
fuperabundance of incorporated coal reduces it almoft to
the ftate of *fonte grife.* It feems, therefore, that charcoal
made of hard wood will give a much greater heat, and, by
precipitating the operation, form the iron ore into metal,
It is fometimes liable to combine a part of its own fubftance with the metal towards the end of the procefs,

by

wood, contained in Corfica, which is propofed to be divided into an exploitation of
forty years ; it would be proper to referve
one tenth, or forty thoufand acres, where

by which means the fteel is found to be more or lefs imperfect. Should, however, this inconvenience exift, is
there no remedy for it? In the fame manner as charcoal
made of oak-holm, and other hard wood, is ufed in the
high forges on account of the fuperior heat it gives, and
the great activity with which its fire melts the ore into
pigs. Charcoal of a fofter quality is referved for the
finery ; that, which is of a ftronger nature might, in the
Catalonian forges, where there is but one fire, be employed, in the beginning of the operation, which is merely
confined to the agglutination of the ore, and raifing the
heat to a proper temper, in order to volatilize the evapo-
rable fubftances, and run the vitrifiable ones into a fufion;
towards the conclufion of the procefs foft coal would fuffice, as nothing remains, at this ftage of the bufinefs, but
to feparate the *oxigene*, which prevents the ferruginous part
from becoming pure metal." Two of the authors of this
Memorial, Meffieurs Vandermonde and Monge, being
confulted, in the prefence of Mr. Lavoifier, on the fuppofed inconvenience attending the ufe of hard coal,
feemed to think thefe fears, or apprehenfions, were chi-
merical or groundlefs; fuppofing, however, the operation
to be properly managed, agreeable to the principles of the
late difcoveries of the art of extracting the iron ore from
it's mine, and of the means of rendering it in the wifhed
for ftate.

the trees might be left ftanding for the term
of eighty years, and the pines may be fuffered to remain even for a longer term. We
fet, likewife, apart in our calculation forty
thoufand acres to fupply the local exigencies
of the inhabitants : thus deducting thefe
forty thoufand acres from the four hundred
thoufand, there remains a refidue of three
hundred and forty thoufand in referve for
exploitation, which being divided into forty
falls, the annual cutting, or clearance,
amounts to eight thoufand five hundred
acres.

Art. II. Wood for Timber and Planks.

The eight thoufand five hundred acres,
which may be annually exploited at fixty-
five cords, the one with the other, will produce five hundred and fifty-two thoufand
cords, or their equivalent. The part of this
wood that may be difpofed of as timber, or
in the piece, and which is fold by the cubic
foot, is merely confined to the very beft
quality, or what is moft perfect throughout
the

the different Cantons, and the quality is by
no means confiderable. The lofty *Makis*,
of which the one-third confifts, yield none.
The oak-holm and cork-trees are very apt to
decay interiorly or rot at heart, and fucceed
not in the growth; and as for the pines,
they grow, for the moſt part, in places ſo
inacceſſible, that the tranſporting the timber
in the piece from off the premiſes would
be attended with greater expence than profit.
It is then computed, that wood diſpoſed of
in this manner cannot exceed one-fixth of
the whole, or the equivalent, of thirty-four
thouſand five hundred cords, which, rated at
about twenty cubic feet, taken promiſcu-
ouſly, the one with the other, in the piece, is
ſuppoſed to be the quantity of found wood,
that may be extracted therefrom, nearly
amounting in bulk to one cord. The produce would then be about fix hundred and
ninety thouſand cubic feet, referved for
timber and planks.

*Art. III. Fuel for Exportation, and the Quan-
tity of Iron that may be annually worked,
with the remainder reduced into Charcoal.*

The portion fet apart for fuel is likewife
confined to what may be advantageoufly
difpofed of in the feveral maritime towns
of Provence, Languedoc, on the coafts of
Nice and Tufcany, in the gulf of Genoa;
and, in fine, the Pope's territory. The
whole amount of what is fold at thefe different markets in the Mediterranean is
vaguely eftimated at a quadruple or quin-
tuple part of the confumption of Marfeilles,
which is fuppofed to be three hundred thoufand weight, or thirty thoufand cords annually; fo that the two above objects,
amounting nearly to the equivalent of one
hundred and eighty cords, to be deducted
from five hundred, fifty-two thoufand, nine
hundred, would ftill leave a refidue of three
hundred and fixty-eight thoufand cords, to
be annually appropriated to the fabrication of
iron. Now, three hundred and fixty-eight
thoufand

thoufand cords, producing three million, fix
hundred, and eighty thoufand quintals of
charcoal, and the Catalonian forges not con-
fuming any more than three pounds and a
half, or at moft four pounds, of charcoal to
each pound of marketable forged iron, it
follows, that fomething more than a million
of quintals of iron may be annually forged in
Corfica.

As the object of exportation is far lefs
profitable than the emolument that would
accrue from home confumption in the iron
manufactories, the hundred and fifty thoufand cords, deftined for the foreign markets,
might alfo be reduced to charcoal, and appropriated to the ufe of forges, which would
prove an additional refource of four hundred
thoufand quintals of charcoal ; but then, it is
a matter of doubt, whether fuch a quantity of
iron, equal to one-half of what Sweden is
known to produce, could be difpofed of
without occafioning a confiderable fall in the
price. It would, perhaps, be more advifeable (inftead of confining the fabrication
                                    merely

merely to raw iron, deftined for exportation in this its unwrought and imperfect ftate) to employ a part of the fuel in giving the iron fome primary form or fhape. This would tend to augment the original value in the difpofing of the faid articles on exportation, as fuel on the fpot is far cheaper than it is in thofe parts where the iron, in its fecond ftate of fabrication, would be marketable.

Art. IV. The Expences attending the Fabrication of Iron.

We fhall hereafter exhibit in full detail, and fhew to demonftration, that the general expences of fabricating iron in Corfica, will never exceed eleven livres per quintal avoirdupois weight. By general expences is meant,

1. The primary purchafe of mineral in the Ifle of Eibe.

2. The freight of the fame, including lading and carriage, to Corfica.

3. The

3. The conveyance by land, which is performed either by teams, or on the backs of mules, to the refpective forges.

4. The making roads, and opening the neceffary paffes.

5. The eftablifhing refervoirs of water for the regular fupply of the channels of the water-pipes, or trompes.

6. The erecting workfhops, fheds, &c. for the forges.

7. The erecting of lodging-houfes and magazines for the accommodation of the artificers and goods.

8. The fabrication of charcoal, and the conveyance of the fame to the forges.

9. The workmen's wages.

10. Beafts of fumpter and land-carriages for the conveyance of forged or fabricated iron to the place of embarkation.

11. The

11. The freight to the moſt conſiderable commercial ports abovementioned, ſituated in the Mediterranean.

12. The ſalary of the ſupernumeraries.

13. The unforeſeen expences.

Now, as the iron of the Iſland of Elbe is reckoned, if not ſuperior, at leaſt equal to the firſt quality · that comes from Sweden and the Province of Biſcay; and as the latter is never rated in this part of Europe worth leſs than eighteen livres per quintal, avoirdupois weight, it is clear, that there will be in Corſica a profit of ſix or ſeven livres upon iron in its rough ſtate, excluſive of what would immediately accrue there-from in its ſecond ſtate of fabrication, which would depend entirely on the non-exportation of fuel to foreign markets, and on the extraordinary ſupply of waters in the Iſland, ſufficient for the working the neceſſary machines or engines. Thus the general profit of Corſican iron may be eſtimated at ſix millions annually.

We

We fhall further demonftrate, that wood for timber and planks, which fells at from forty to feventy fols the cubic foot, bears a profit of at leaft twenty fols per cubic foot; and that the fix hundred and ninety thoufand cubic feet, which Corfica can thus furnifh, will produce more than fix hundred and ninety thoufand livres clear profit.

It will likewife appear in the fequel, that fire-wood exported, which always fells in Provence from fifty to fixty fols per weight (the tenth part of a cord), bearing above one livre profit per weight; the five hundred and fifty thoufand cords that may be appropriated to this ufe, producing one million five hundred thoufand weight, would yield above a million five hundred thoufand livres.

Thus the three articles abovementioned, viz. forged iron, wood for timber, and fuel, will evidently produce above eight millions.

Now, as the faid profit of eight millions implies a fecondary emolument, at leaft double the amount, which would tend to

the

the general advantage of the country, the refult of the whole is an acquifition to fociety exceeding four and twenty millions annually, whether termed value, produce, labour, or emolument.

Be it obferved, that thefe advantages accrue from the application of general induftry to objects hitherto difregarded and totally neglected.

SECTION IV.

Art. 1. A detailed Application of this Syftem confined to the Exploitation of one particular Canton.

IN order to give a juft idea of the expence and profit attending the due exploitation of the feveral forts of wood that grow in Corfica, we will now apply, in a detailed manner, this general fyftem, to one particular Canton ; on which fpot it is propofed to allow a fingle company of adventurers, that chufe to embark in the undertaking, to make

the

the experiment, at their own coft and rifk, whether of profit or lofs. Their effay will ferve as an example for the encouragement of the reft of Corfica. Locality may, un-doubtedly, caufe fome variation as to the application of this plan, in the different parts of the Ifland, which are more or lefs ftocked with wood, which are more or lefs acceffible; in fine, which are more or leis diftinct from the fea-coaft. It is, however, poffible, by a trial of this nature, to form an adequate idea of this bufinefs. Refults better calculated will be obtained by analogy, than by the vague reckonings of fimple theory.

Art. II. Domaine of Galeria.

The territory propofed for exploitation forms a part of a certain jurifdiction of ninety-one thoufand acres of land belonging to the crown, known by the name of the *Domaine of Galeria*, fituated on the weftern coaft of the Ifland, 15,000 toifes to the fouth of Fort Calvy, which is the neareft inhabited

L 3   fpot.

fpot. It reaches eaftward from the fea to
the foot of the mountains of Niolo, that lie
weftward, bearing a like extent of nearly
fifteen thoufand toifes.

In this direction, which is that of its
greateft dimenfion, this territory is divided
in two nearly equal parts by the river, or
torrent, Santa Maria della Spofata, formed
by the feveral waters that pafs through the
Gorges (ftraits), which compofe the beach or
Concha of *Galeria*. The heights, that bound
the *Concha*, being in the form of a long extended horfe-fhoe, terminate in the gulf of
Galeria, where there is a tolerable fafe harbour, fufceptible of great improvement at
little or no expence. In its prefent ftate,
this bay is fufficiently capacious to receive
fecond-rate merchantmen. This Canton is
nearly the hundred and fortieth part of the
whole fuperficies of Corfica, and contains
about the fortieth part of its woods *.

The

* It may not be improper to give here a fhort Hiftory of
this Domaine; as it was the occafion of a difpute, that will
be

The river Galeria, or della Spofata, at
the diftance of nearly four thoufand five
hun-

be neceffarily fubmitted to the decifion of the National
Affembly by its Committee of Crown Lands. In the year
1704, the Republic of Genoa had granted as a Copyhold to
a Nobleman, called *Luigi Sauli*, the lands of *Paratella, Mar-
folino, Galeria, Filaforma,* and *Sia,* that contain an extent of
territory of ninety-one thoufand acres, now called the
Domaine of Galeria. The conditions of this Copyhold-
Tenure were to build habitations to a certain amount, and
eftablifh a certain number of Colonifts, with the exprefs
claufe of forfeiture, after a few years, upon the non-per-
formance of the abovementioned conditions. Not a fingle
article of the agreement was fulfilled, on account of the
oppofition formed by the inhabitants of the *Pieve de Niolo,*
as is afferted by thofe who are in the poffeffion of the rights
of the late Luigi Sauli. Be it as it will, the Republic of
Genoa, in 1709, declared the right of Copyhold forfeited ;
and, in 1717, granted the faid lands to the inhabitants of the
aforefaid neighbouring *Pieve.* The terms of this new Copyhold were very fimple and eafy ; confifting only in the payment of a Canonic Fee of four hundred livres, Genoefe
money, making nearly three hundred and twenty livres,
French. This new grant was, however, fubject to immediate forfeiture on the non-payment of the faid fee for two
fucceffive years.

It does not appear that the Niolins ever paid this fee,
and ever fince the year 1729 they have been almoft at perpetual war with their then Sovereign. Thus have they continued

L 4

hundred toifes from the place where it
empties itfelf into the fea, previous to its
water-

tinued to enjoy their forfeited Copyhold by force, which,
agreeable to the conditions of the tenure, they had loft all
right to long before the infurrection in 1729.

During a calm in 1751, the power of the Republic being
then in full vigour, a new Act of Copyhold was paffed concerning the Lands of Galeria. They were again granted
to the *Pieve de Niolo*, fubject to the fame claufes and exac-
tions as in 1717. The Niolins made good their payments
the two firft years ; but, in the year 1756, upon the breaking out of a frefh infurrection, they neglected to pay the
ftipulated contract, although there were feveral intervals of
tranquillity from that time to 1768 and 1769, when France
became poffeffed of this Ifland. In 1771, the re-union of
this Domaine to the Crown was declared and fince accepted
by the *Pieve de Niolo*, which tranfcribed this regulation
upon the Regifter of their Community in 1773, requefting
only of the Superintendant of the Crown Lands the liberty
of pafture for their cattle, offering to pay a certain fum in
lieu of arrears. They further made a tender of paying
annually, in future, the fum of four hundred livres, Frençh,
till Government fhould think proper to difpofe of thefe
lands by frefh grants, for which they (the inhabitants of
the Pieve) would folicit. The Superintendant at the fame
time promifed to back their Petition. This Agent was
afterwards difavowed by Government. The Niolins never
paid but nine hundred livres, being the one-half of what
the arrears were rated at ; and, notwithftanding they offered

to

watering the plain, paffes immediately
betwixt two rocks perpendicularly cut,
thirty-

to pay annually the current Canonic Fees, they have totally
neglected to fulfil this voluntary obligation. Being in the
actual enjoyment of the feveral advantages derivable from
the poffeffion of the premifes, the inhabitants of the *Pieve*
fhould have made good their feveral payments, in order to
ftop all purfuit on the part of the plaintiff; but they pretended, or alledged, as a pretext for their not fulfilling this,
their contract, that the Superintendant had not prefented
them with the ratification of the act (by Government) to
which they had fubfcribed.

In 1785, Adminiftration made a grant of Lands upon this
Domaine, having previoufly done the fame with refpect to
feveral Forefts. Hereupon the Heir of Mr. Luigi Sauli, of
Genoa, at the inftigation of a hungry lawyer at Baftia, inftead of commencing a fuit with the Republic, or claiming
an indemnification for the having defeized him of a grant
made in favour of his Father, commenced an immediate
profecution againft the King's Domaine. Now, as the
Niolins entered into the enjoyment of the Copyhold of this
Domaine only in 1717, and afterwards in 1751, on the
Republic's declaring the late Mr. Luigi Sauli to be in a
ftate of forfeiture, they likewife became intermediate
parties, and propofe hereafter to prove, as principals in the
profecution, that they have not forfeited their right of poffeffion, notwithftanding they had violated every article of
the agreement, and they account for their not fulfilling the
fame in a plaufible manner indeed!

The

thirty-fix feet in height, the diftance between being alfo about fix and thirty feet ; and it is through

The Pieve de Niolo has a population of three thoufand fouls, and poffeffes a prodigious number of cattle, but particularly of goats. According to its fyftem of rural œconomy, a vaft tract is requifite to procure the neceffary pafture. This is the reafon why the inhabitants are fo defirous of preferving the full enjoyment of the territory of Galeria, which contains, as has been already obferved, ninety-one thoufand acres, exclufive of the forty thoufand that are contained in the Pieve. But is this fyftem of rural œconomy (which is confined to the increafe of goats, and to the culture of a few acres for barley, in the proportion of two to a thoufand at moft) the beft and moft advantageous of all? And becaufe the Niolins would perhaps be enabled to breed and feed double the number of goats on a tract of double the extent, fhould thefe lands be given up to them, and every other means of improvement they are fufceptible of neglected? In what country are goats permitted to graze in the plains and fertile uplands? Are they not, on the contrary, every where confined to the fummits and places of difficult accefs? Thefe animals therefore feed where no other culture could be attended to, that would turn to a better account. Ought, in fine, the State to be deprived of the ufe and value of the extenfive forefts and woods which this Canton contains, merely to gratify the wifhes of the inhabitants of the *Pieve*, who defire the exclufive privilege of poffeffing alone the Domaine of Galeria? Befides, have they either the inclination or the means to avail themfelves of the grant, fhould it be given in their favour?

through this opening the waters run, that pafs over an extent of forty thoufand acres, or forty million of fquare toifes, allowing for what the earth abforbs. Now, as there is in Corfica a fall of thirty-three or thirty-four inches depth of water, proceeding from the fnows or rain ; and as the abforption of the waters is not one-half here to what it is in France, perhaps not above one quarter, on account of the nature of the foil and the fteep declivities of the adjacent grounds, which

favour? It is thought not. If, however, it be any ways interefting to procure to the *Pieve de Niolo* fome addition to their pafture-grounds; it is, at the fame time, infinitely advantageous not to include, in the faid grant, woods, that may be particularly beneficial to the Adminiftration of Corfica, and the public at large.

Such are the facts and queftions which the National Affembly will, *in its wifdom*, have to decide upon, relative to the Domaine of Galeria. As the inquiry is rather of a political than a judicial nature, it is highly important the Affembly fhould determine the matter, if it wifhes to fee the falutary effects that would accrue from the exploitation of the woods in Corfica. The fyftem propofed would foon put the country in fuch a flourifhing ftate, as to enable it fhortly to ceafe being burthenfome to the State.

are

are no where three thoufand toifes diftant
from the bed of the river; it follows, that there
pafs, through this kind of aperture, about
eight million cubic feet of water, which are
nearly the three-fourths of four myriads of
cubic feet, which fall in the courfe of the year,
divided by three hundred and fixty-five days,
or about one hundred cubic feet of water
per fecond. The fact is, that at this paffage,
there is always a depth of one foot of water,
and a breadth of fix and thirty, and that
in the greateft droughts; but in the winter,
on the melting of the fnows, or the fall of
heavy rains, the waters frequently rife to a
height of twenty feet.

It may be here obferved, that nature
feems to point out this fpot as peculiarly
adapted to the forming a firft and principal refervoir, as it would be neither difficult nor expenfive to command the neceffary waters for a fimilar eftablifhment.

In order to effect this, it is propofed entirely to dam up the river of Galeria at the
place

place where it paffes in a body between two
parallel rocks, which, as it has been already
obferved, are thirty fix feet high, and at a
fimilar diftance from each other. A little
above this dam a canal may be formed thirty
feet wide and five feet deep, and made to
flow a line per toife downwards, and that
for the continued length of 100 toifes round
a fmall ravin, the ftream of which empties
itfelf into the river Galeria, in the vicinity
of the two rocks; and it is at the extremity
of the ravin, and near the principal river,
where the forges, workfhops, &c. fhould
be erected. It would be advifeable to erect
thefe buildings in fuch a manner, that there
might be nothing to apprehend from the
impetuofity of the water; fhould the Torrent de la Spofata exceed it's natural bounds,
and deftroy the precautionary works raifed,
by human prudence and forefight, in order
to contain it within due limits; the neceffary materials being on the fpot, the works
fhould be erected as folid as poffible. By
means of this dyke the furface of the river,
fenced in on every fide where the waters

are

are higheft, will be raifed thirty feet where they are loweft. This will furnifh the feveral pipes with a regular fupply of a hundred cubic feet of water each fecond *.

Art.

---

* It would have been an object highly worthy the attention of naturalifts to have minutely obferved the wonderful effect produced in the infide of the *Trompes*, and occafioned by the fall of the water, from whence there arifes a current of air, the intenfenefs of which is but very imperfectly meafured. It is not certain, that the moifture or damp air, which paffes through the wind-pipe does not, when decompofed, furnifh by contact, with the fire in the crucible, a portion of vital air, that enters about fourfifths into the compofition of the water. No one yet has been able to afcertain, whether the water, by its fall into the windcafe, does not, in fome meafure, decompofe the atmofpherical air which it draws with it; whether the vital part of atmofpherical air is not rather drawn towards the pipe, whereas the water that feparates would, at the fame time, attract the other aerial fluids of the common air, more fufceptible, perhaps, of being attracted by it? or, in fine, whether the effect produced may not be juft the contrary? There is no fure way of afcertaining which has the greater influence either upon the body of air that paffes into the tube, or upon the nature of the air itfelf; whether it is the height the water falls from, and it's proportionate velocity, or the quantity of water falling from a lefs height. The fact, explained, more or lefs thoroughly as to circumftances, is, that air is conveyed

into

Art. III. The several sorts of Wood growing in this Canton particularised, and the quantity ascertained.

The wood, in this select quarter of the domain of Galeria, may cover an extent of ten thousand acres, or a ninth part of the surface of the whole domain, viz. five thousand acres of lofty makis, or coppice, four thousand acres of forest trees, and a thousand acres of larch pines. The makis, which generally occupy the bottoms or

into the channel of the pipe by the fall of water that enters the body of the *trompe*; there must, therefore exist a necessary proportion between the diameter of the pipe's *orifice* and that of the body of the *trompe* and the height the *water* falls from. All these particulars must be previously ascertained, and it is absolutely impossible to carry on a complicated operation, and execute it in a satisfactory manner, unless one has such a perfect knowledge of the several elements, which influence during the process, so as to be able to modify the said operation accordingly. Without this previous information, the naturalist is reduced to the condition of an ignorant mechanic; who, from frequent observations, will often have the advantage over him, whose principles are not the immediate result of accurate and exact calculation.

lower

lower grounds, are a mixture of the following trees :—The arbutus, privet, turpentine,
birch, fmall oak-holm, juniper and the wild
olive. The foreft trees, which grow on the
femi-heights chiefly confift in the large oak-
holm, which the Italians call *leccio*, a few
beech-trees, but a far greater quantity of
the better fort of afh, befides the pine, which
is found on the higher flats, and on the
fummits.

The produce of thefe different forts of
wood may, as we have obferved above, be
computed at fixty five cords per acre; therefore ten thoufand acres may be rated at fix
hundred and fifty thoufand cords.

*Art. IV. The different ufes the feveral forts of
Wood may be put to.*

By dividing the exploitation of the Canton into forty yearly falls, the annual
clearance would fomewhat exceed fixteen
thoufand cords, or the produce of two hundred and fifty acres. The wood might be
deftined

deftined to the following purpofes. The amount of two thoufand cords might be fet apart for timber and planks, which would give forty thoufand cubic feet, at twenty cubic feet per cord; fix thoufand cords might be deftined for firing which make fixty thoufand weight of Marfeilles, confift-ing of four quintals (table weight, or three quintals and a quarter avoirdupoife); and, in fine, eight thoufand cords might be con-verted into charcoal, which, at ten quintals per cord, would produce eighty thoufand quintals of this fort of combuftible ; a quan-tity fully fufficient to work from twenty thoufand to twenty four thoufand quintals of iron, in following the procefs of the Ca-talonian forges.

Art. V. Carriage-Roads.

The woods, in this part of Corfica, com-mence at four thoufand toifes from the fea, and extend as far as ten thoufand toifes up the country. Being at a diftance of feven thou-fand toifes from the fea, and upon the River

de

de la Spofata, you will find yourfelf in the
very centre of a circle, bearing a radius of
three thoufand toifes covered, more or lefs,
with wood; fo that feven thoufand toifes
are the middle ratio of the refpective dif-
tances for the land carriage, or conveyance
to the different ports, and confequently for
the feveral roads or cuts that might be annually made, at the rate of two thoufand
toifes yearly.

Art. VI. Expences of the Roads.

The company engaged in exploiting the
foreft of Lonca (for the marine fervice) not
very far diftant from Galeria, has made feveral roads for carriages, and *fliding* ones
(gliffoires) that penetrate from nine to ten
thoufand toifes up into the interior parts of
this foreft. The hurdle roads (gliffoires)
are ufeful for the conveying large pieces of
timber, fifty two feet long by twenty two.

The faid timber weighs near upon 10,000
pound weight, and it's principal ufe is to
form

form beams for fhips of the line : thefe roads, excepting the flides, never coft more than forty fols per toife, being in width from twelve to fifteen feet. Now, notwithftand- ing, the nature of the ground is every where nearly alike, we fhall hereafter allow fix livres per toife for the roads of Galeria, and that for the three following reafons :

1ft. On account of their width being eighteen feet.

2dly, Small bridges are neceffary over the rivulets in the narrow paffes ; and

3dly, There is a neceffity of making roads, that are to laft forty years, more folid than temporary ones, in the woods, where they are only wanted for the term of two years.

Art. VII. The proper Perfons to be employed in the bufinefs of making and repairing the Roads, are the following :

The Lucchefe, Parmefans, and Romag- nols, together with other Italian peafants,

M 2   who,

who, forming a body of three or four thoufand labourers, arrive annually in Corfica,
towards the month of October, where they
continue till May. They are handy and
diligent at every kind of work: and might,
therefore, be advantageoufly employed in
making and repairing the roads. The
natives fhould, however, have the preference, and it is *only* on their declining the
tafk that foreigners fhould be employed.
This is frequently the cafe, for the Corfican
peafants prefer tending their cattle, befides
they do not feem fit for work of the kind.
The Lucchefe, &c. take away with them
from Corfica annually, a confiderable fum
in fpecie, amounting to more than three
hundred thoufand livres.

Out of the four thoufand toifes, from the
fea to where the woods begin, there exift
already carriage roads for three fourths of
the way, that is to fay, three thoufand
toifes; confequently nothing further would
be requifite the firft year but to make a thoufand toife of new road, and three thoufand

of hurdle ditto, in all four thoufand toifes, which two hundred Lucchefe could eafily accomplifh in the fpace of a month; this work would coft three livres the toife, or twelve thoufand livres in the whole, and three fmall bridges would coft a fimilar fum of twelve thoufand livres. Thus the total expence for the roads made the firft year would amount to twenty four thoufand livres. The fubfequent expences would not amount to more than twelve thoufand livres annually, allowing for two thoufand toifes, and including the repairs of the roads already made.

Art. VIII. The conveniency of carriage conveyance compared with that by beafts of Sumpter.

Hitherto the fole mode of conveyance from place to place has been, in Corfica, on the backs of mules. This practice has long prevailed in the country. The neceffity, however, of adopting a fpeedy and more economical conveyance, points out the pro-

priety

priety of giving the preference to carriage conveyance. This requires the eſtabliſh-ment of good roads. Nay the ſucceſs of the undertaking abſolutely depending on this improvement, it is an indiſpenſible meaſure.

The proportion between the ſervice per-formed by a horſe, or mule, that drags in a cart, &c. and one that carries his burthen on his back is more than four to one ; thus, confining one's obſervation to the weight alone of what is to be carried, there is al-ready a difference of three hundred per cent. in favour of carriage conveyance, making a reaſonable allowance for the occaſional re-pairs of the roads and carriages, which al-ways correſpond to the weight or load con-veyed : this is, however, a trifling charge, and will require but a ſlight deduction. Another important obſervation is, that wood proves more or leſs valuable as it is more or leſs voluminous; now this advantage is loſt by the conveyance on the backs of mules, as each piece of timber muſt not ex-ceed one hundred and twenty five pound weight, which is half a load.

An

An example taken on the fpot will ferve to make this exceedingly clear. The company of Lonca pays to Government forty fols for each larch pine, from fix to fourteen feet round, and from forty to feventy high. By means of the roads which have been made, at the expence of one hundred and fifty livres, veffel beams are with eafe conveyed from off the premifes, that, one with the other, fetched at Toulon four hundred and fifty livres ; whereas a tree, of the fame dimenfions, conveyed on the back of a mule, will coft feventy five livres, and produce no more than a hundred livres in planks.

It is obferved, that the principal or main road wanted in this quarter, confifts in a ftrait line of four thoufand toifes, following pretty clofely the courfe of the river that has an eaftward and weftward bearing. The afcent is fo eafy that it fcarce can be perceived, and the whole length of the ground is nearly clear of rocks.

Art.

Art. IX. Of Wainage, or Carriage.

We have remarked above, that the diftance of conveyance · is nearly equal from
and to the feveral different points, being
about feven thoufand toifes, as well from the
port to the forefts, where the iron mineral
is fituated, as from the forefts to the port,
where the forged and wrought iron, together
with the wood, are to be fhipped off for exportation. This diftance, going and coming,
is nearly what the overfeers, or infpectors,
of the roads, caufeways, and bridges, moft
commonly rate one day's teamage at. A double yoke of oxen would fuffice to each team
in Corfica : they would have to draw only
three thoufand pounds weight from the
forefts down to the port, and five hundred
weight lefs up from the port to the interior
parts. The objects to be drawn would confift in fixty thoufand weight of fire wood,
which, at three quintals and a quarter avoir-

dupois, would be each . . . 210,000

Forty thoufand cubic feet of wood
for timber or planks, which, as
to weight and bulk, are equal to
feven thoufand four hundred
weight, or twenty four thoufand
quintals, which form . . . 24,000

Twenty thoufand quintals of forged
iron 20,000
_____

Total of the weight to be carried 254,000

These two hundred and fifty four thoufand quintals make about eight thoufand five
hundred loads, at thirty quintals per load,
which it will take three hundred days
journey to convey; and this may be done
by twenty eight or thirty teams at moft,
drawn by a double yoke of oxen.

N. B. No allowance has been made of
the iron ore by land from the port to the
forges, becaufe this may be effected without
any expence, as the teams or carts that
ferved to convey the wood and iron to the
place

place of embarkation, would otherwife return empty. On thefe occafions the teams
would not be heavily laden, having only
one eighth of their ordinary load.

Art. X. The Freight.

The two hundred and fifty four thoufand
quintals, to be conveyed by fea, would, on
the whole, form fixty three or fixty four
feparate cargoes for the hoys, (alleges, or
large tartanes) of fifteen hundred burthen,
which are equivalent to four thoufand quin-
ta's avoirdupois. As thefe cargoes would
be principally deftined for the port of Marfeilles, they might be fhipped aboard feven
hoys, which will eafily perform nine voyages from Corfica to Provence during the
year. The veffels might even go three
voyages more, as the cargoes are always
ready, and the lading may be effected in
eight and forty hours. But limiting our
calculation to nine annual voyages; each
hoy will have forty days remaining to perform a voyage of eighty leagues in, to un-
load

load their cargoes and return. Each voyage going and coming do not require more than four days for loading and unloading. So that there remain thirty six days, time fufficient, to perform another voyage of eighty leagues, and allowing for the return of the veffel, which has, or may be fuppofed to have failed one hundred and fixty leagues: an allowance for this extra voyage is, however, only made on the fuppofition of the fhip's not being detained in port by contrary winds. This allowance is two thirds more than is requifite for fo fhort a voyage, which is fometimes performed in two days: and the more efpecially, if feven fhips are employed in the fame direction, and at the fame time, either going or coming, the wind when unfavourable to the one will prove favourable to the other, fo that the fwift failing of the one will make ample amends for the tardy progrefs of the other; and, in fine, the crofs winds would ferve the purpofe of both.

N. B. It has been already remarked, that the conveying the iron mineral from
the

the Ifle of Elbe to Corfica will coft nothing,
and therefore no additional charge has been
made for this particular article; and that
for this reafon, the bottoms, that ferve to
convey wood and iron from Corfica to Provence, returning for the moft part to Corfica
in ballaft; fome of them would from
time to time, touch at the Ifle of Elbe,
and take in cargoes of iron ore. Ten voyages out of the fixty three would amply
fuffice for this bufinefs. Each cargo would
confift of four thoufand quintals of mineral,
making in the whole forty thoufand quintals which is more than fufficient for the
manufacturing of twenty thoufand quintals
of iron.

*Art. XI. A detailed Lift of the different
Artificers and Workmen employed in this
Exploitation.*

The eftablifhment intended, by way of
effay, is to be formed on a deferted and uncultivated piece of ground, at fix leagues
diftance from any fixed habitation, where
there would be neither the means of pro-
curing

curing the neceſſary hands, nor food for the ſupport of the workmen employed ; it will be neceſſary to collect together on the ſame ſpot, forgemen, colliers, carpenters, maſons, joiners, ſmiths, wheel-wrights, harneſs-makers and ſadlers ; carmen, bakers, chaplain, ſurgeon and attendants on the ſick, ſtore-keepers and warehouſe-men, comptroller, clerks, &c. amounting, in the whole, to two hundred perſons.

Art. XII. Accommodations for the Workmen and Store-houſes.

A ſquare building, of twenty-ſix toiſes in front, incloſing a court of eight toiſes ſquare, two ſtories high, with ſtore-rooms over the cellars and ground-floors, would ſuffice for the accommodating two hundred men with lodging, &c. A building of this deſcription would allow of forty-eight thouſand ſquare feet for lodging, excluſive of cellars and garrets. Now, as forty-four feet ſquare would be ſufficient for the lodging each artificer, the one with the other, the two hundred would occupy twenty eight thouſand

eight

eight hundred fquare feet on the two upper
ftories; the furplus being nearly twenty
thoufand fquare feet, might be referved for
warehoufes and workfhops, exclufive of
what would be requifite for the manufacturing the iron. It is calculated, that a
fimilar edifice would require two thoufand
two hundred cannes of two hundred and
fifty cubic pans of mafonry, or eleven hundred cubic toifes. This would coft on the
fpot, materials and labour included, fixty
livres per toife; otherwife, for the eleven
hundred toifes, fixty-fix thoufand livres; and
as the mafon-work of fuch a building would
be very fimple and plain, it might amount to
fomething more than one-third of the whole
charge; it follows therefore that the propofed edifice would coft one hundred and
eighty thoufand livres.

Art. XIII. Temporary Barracks.

The expence of erecting a building of
this extent in Corfica is not the only obftacle,
as it would be in any other part of France.

To

To erect in the Domaine of Galeria, a mere defert of more than fix leagues diameter, and diftant from the fea-fhore four thoufand toifes, a building on the above conftruction, it will require four months at leaft to collect the neceffary number of workmen, amounting to two hundred ; thefe different artificers muft be lodged and put under cover from the moment of their arrival.   For this purpofe it is propofed to befpeak at Marfeilles four and twenty barracks, of eighteen feet fquare each, and fifteen high to the roof; the fame to confift of two ftories. Thefe barracks, conftructed upon the perfect model of thofe of the Pioneers, that work at the *Butte de l'Etoile,* on the road to Neuilly and in the environs of Verfailles. Thefe barracks are eafily taken to pieces, being formed of rafters and fliding planks ; they admit of twelve men each; viz. fix men on a ftory, and are fixed up in four and twenty hours.

A barrack of the fort is compofed of twelve dozen rafters of three inches fquare, and

the

sliding planks of one foot one, the whole
nine feet in length : thefe rafters and planks
coft eight livres the dozen, and will come to
four and twenty livres, iron and workman-
ship included. So that the fifteen dozen,
that a barrack fit to contain twelve men is
compofed of, will, upon the whole, coft
three hundred and fixty livres; and the
twenty-four barracks made complete at Marfeilles would come to eight thoufand fix
hundred livres.

A dozen of this fpecies of planks and
rafters form nine cubic feet, which, at forty-
four or forty-five pound weight the cubic
foot, weigh about four hundred pounds.
Each barrack will weigh fixty quintals;
therefore the twenty-four, taken collectively,
will amount to one thoufand four hundred
and forty quintals; which will, on account
of the fpace they occupy, more than on account of the weight, require two moderate
fized *Tartanes*. The freighting of the two
will come to eight hundred livres.

The

The land-carriage from the port to the above indicated ſpot, which is four thouſand toiſes diſtance up the country, might be performed by ſix team, of four oxen each, (forming eight days journey), as there exiſts already a road for wheel-carriages the whole length of the way. There is, however, about one thouſand toiſes of the way bad ; that is, where it paſſes through the bed of the river. The road here conſiſts of large pebble-ſtones, lodged by the current of the water. But this conveyance may be eaſily effected by mules. To carry one thouſand four hundred and forty quintals, would be a journey of two hundred and eighty-eight days for the mules, at two journies per day, and two quintals and a half per journey. Two mules and their driver coſt four livres per day. They are eaſy to be had in the neighbourhood ; the carriage, therefore, will be effected in eight days, by thirty-ſix mules, and will coſt about ſix hundred livres. In fine, it follows, that each barrack capable of lodging twelve men, together with the carrying and fixing expences,

N   will

will amount nearly to four hundred and
thirty livres, and the twenty-four to fomething more than ten thoufand livres.

It muft be obferved, in order to afford
accommodation, for fuppofing 200 workmen, that only fixteen barracks are abfolutely neceffary, though the calculation was
fixed at twenty-four: the other eight will
ferve for the locking up of the tools and
provifions. After the conftruction of the
above building, thefe barracks not being
very expenfive, may be eafily increafed
afterwards if wanted. They will ferve as
ftationary boxes in the woods, where workmen are, employed, or wherefoever new
conftructions are neceffary.

SECTION V.

Art. I. Expences Extraordinary and Annual.

The expences of this eftablifhment may
be divided into two claffes, the *firft* of primary advances, the fecond clafs contains the
annual difburfements.

FIRST

FIRST CLASS.

Art. II. The Extraordinary Expences are

1. For the roads and bridges.

2. For temporary barracks.

3. For lodging houfes and magazines.

4. For the conftruction of the forges, and the making a canal for fupplying the pipes with water.

5. For the purchafing oxen and carriages for land fervice.

6. For the furnifhing of *boys* (*alleges* or *tartanes*) for the fea fervice.

The above expences are eftimated as follow:

For the making roads a length of
    4,000 toifes, and three fmall
    bridges, will, at three livres per
    toife for the roads, and at 4,000
    livres each bridge, amount in
    the whole, as has been already
    ftated 24,000

Twenty

Brought over Livres (French) 24,000

Twenty-four temporary barracks
at 430 livres each, on delivery at
the place of deftination, will coft 10,320

The erecting dwellings for the
workmen, together with the neceffary ftorehoufes 180,000

To work 20,000 quintals of iron,
fix Catalonian forges will fuffice;
which, together, with the expence of making a canal for the
general conveyance of water to
all the pipes will coft . . . 96,000

We have already obferved, that
the weight of thefe different articles, which are to be conveyed
by land carriage, will amount to
254,000 quintals, and require 28
teams, to be drawn by four oxen
each. To this, fhould be added

Livres 310,320

the

Brought over Livres   310,320

the carriage alfo from the coal works to the forges of 72,0co quintals of charcoal, neceſſary for working 20,000 quintals of iron, which will require four carriages more, in all 32 teams. But to be ſure of anſwering every exigency of this ſervice, 36 carriages and 144 oxen are abſolutely neceſſary. This at 150 livres each carriage, makes   5,400

And 150 livres for the purchafe of each ox may be rated at . *.   21,600

This forms a Total of Livres   337,320

OBSERVATION.

Tuſcany will furniſh the neceſfary oxen, which are far preferable to horſes and mules, becauſe they

     are

are cheaper and are kept at lefs expence. Befides in cafe of accidents,
or age, thefe animals have an in-
trinfic value.

The freight for fea conveyance
requires feven *alleges* or large
tartanes (hoys) which will coft
18,000 livres each : this makes
altogether , ... 126,000

Add thereto the fum of . . . 337,320

*And the Total Amount of primary
Expences will be* 463,320

N. B. Although the purchafe of feven
hoys is here made to amount to the fum of
126,000 livres; the expence may be avoided,
not being abfolutely neceffary. For fhould
it be thought preferable to hire *tartanes*, the
freight would then fall within the annual
expences, which will reduce the primary
ones

ones to 337,320 livres. Yet upon fecond confideration, it is certainly more advantageous to have veffels belonging to the eftablifhment. In fine, fhould it be determined on to make this primary advance, the feamen's wages muft be deducted, and added to the account of the annual difburfements.

Art. III. Annual Expence.

The expences are,

1. The intereft of the capital of extraordinary charges of the primary eftablifhment.

2. The making the neceffary roads for facilitating and forwarding the bufinefs in general of exploiting the woods in Corfica.

3. The purchafe of ore in the ifland of Elbe.

4. The making of charcoal.

5. The wages of the artificers, and other workmen at the forges.

6. The wages of the wood cutters, fellers, hewers, and fawyers.

N 4

7 The

7. The carmen, or team drivers' wages.

8. The keep of the neceſſary cattle.

9. The ſeamen's wages.

10. The wages of the overſeers and an allowance for the different unforeſeen expences.

Art. IV. Intereſt of the primary advances.

The intereſt of the capital employed in primary diſburſements ought to be rated at 10 per cent. or conſidered as a ſunk capital. For there are ſeveral of the objects, upon which it is advanced, that are liable to caſualties, being of a periſhable nature, ſuch as carriages, cattle, and ſhipping. On the other hand the buildings, forges, canals, and roads are not ſo liable to injury, and therefore conſtitute a real and ſolid capital fund, durable and permanent in

it's

it's nature; fo that upon the whole, the annual expence fhould not be rated at lefs than . . 60,000

Art. V. The Roads.

Allowing 2,000 toifes for the an-, nual continuation of the new roads, which rated at fix livres per toife will be 12,000

Art. VI. The Ore.

The mineral of the ifland of Elbe yielding more than fifty pounds of forged iron per quintal; and the intended fabrication, being to the amount of 20,000 quintals, there will be a demand for 40,000 quintals of ore, which, at 24 fols per quintal, will coft . . . 48,000

REMARK.

In confideration of the vaft con-

Livres 120,000

fumption

fumption of ore, it is highly probable the original proprietors of
this mineral fubftance may, on due
reprefentation, make a confiderable
diminution in the price. The confumption of this article will be rather more than lefs.

Art. VII. The Charcoal.

The making of charcoal cofts 10
fols per quintal, or 100 fols per
cord, which will give ten quintals of charcoal, viz. two fols for
the cutting down and difpofing
of a fufficient quantity of wood
to form a quintal, or 20 fols,
per cord; four fols for carriage
to the coal works; and four fols
more for the converting the
wood into charcoal, or 40 fols
per cord. In order to make
20,000 quintals of iron, the con-

120,000

fumption

Brought over Livres   120,000

fumption of charcoal will be
72,000 quintals: therefore this
article will coft upon the whole⹁ 36,000

Art. VIII. The Artificers, or Work-
    men, at the Forges.

It will require fix forges to make
  20,000 quintals of iron, and eight
  men to each forge ; in all 48 men
  at 40 fols per day, the one with
  the other; and it is calculated that
  the whole-work will take up the
  fpace of 300 days labour   28,800

Art. IX. The Wood-Cutters, Fel-
  lers, Hewers, and Sawyers.

Thefe woodmen are to cut up a
  quantity of wood on the premifes, equal to 8,000 cords, ap-
  propriating the fame to its different ufes, as has been already

           Livres   184,800
                 obferved.

Brought over Livres   184,800

obferved. This work would require 45: viz. ten wood-cutters, twenty fellers, and fifteen faw-yers, for 300 days; which at 40 fols per day, the one with the other, will coft   27,000

N. B. The cutting down and dif-poſing of the wood deftined for firing, cofts 30 fols per cord; the timber fit for houfe and ſhip-building, or for planks, cofts fel-ling, hewing, and fawing the pines, three fols per cubic foot; the oak-holms, five fols, or upon an average of four fols per cubic foot. Sawing cofts 10 fols per cubic foot, when the wood is reduced into fmall planks, or fmall parcels; but fix only, if the planks are thicker, or parcels larger.

Livres   211,800

Art.

Brought over Livres   211,000

Art. X. The Carmen, or Team Drivers.

The 36 carmen, or drivers for the
32 teams, at 30 fols per day, will
coft, per annum, or for 300 days
work   16,200

Art. XI. The keep of the Cattle.

The keep of 44 oxen, at twelve fols
per day, will coft annually . 31,526

IMPORTANT REMARK.

In regard to this article it is proper to obferve, that the totality of
this expence would only take place
for the firft or fecond year at moft;
and it is evident that one third of
the above charge might be appropriated to the culture of natural

Livres 258,726

or

or artificial meadows, where the
foil is good. This would furnifh
the neceffary provender, which has
hitherto been imported from Arles,
in Provence, on account of the
very great fcarcity of this article in
Corfica.

Art. XII. The Seamen's wages.

The hoys of 1,500 burden each,
     amounting to three thoufand
     quintals of Provence weight, or
     four thoufand avoirdupois, re-
     quire for working each veffel a
     crew of nine men ; viz.
     A Captain at 150 livres per month
     A Mate   80 do.   do.
     Six Sailors   40 do.   do.
     A Cabin boy 30 do.   do.
     The whole makes 500 livres
     per month, or 6,000 livres per
     annum. Thus the feven Tar-

Livres   258,726

tanes

Brought over Livres   258,726

tanes neceffary for this fervice
would coft yearly   42,000

It has been already mentioned,
that the feven veffels, this fervice
would neceffarily require, could
perform nine voyages yearly from
Corfica to Provence, and return
as often; in the whole we may
reckon 126 voyages. Suppofing
the company, as we faid before,
fhould wifh to avoid making a
primary advance of 126,000
livres, the purchafe money for
the faid veffels, and fhould prefer to take in pay large traders,
the freight of thefe veffels, which
carry about 200 ton, will coft,
per voyage, at leaft, 800 livres
per veffel. According to this calculation the 126 voyages will coft
100,800 livres annually--where-
as, they may be brought to coft

Livres   300,726

no

no more than 42,000 livres per
annum : this, together with the
intereſt of 126,000 livres, would
make a conſiderable ſaving, by
having veſſels of one's own. The
intereſt would, at leaſt, amount
to 50,000 livres per annum.

*Art. XIII. The wages for the
Overſeers, &c.*

Beſides blackſmiths, fellers, hewers, ſawyers, and drivers, there
would be an indiſpenſable neceſſity of engaging for directing
and ſuperintending the different
departments in this extenſive undertaking, (beſides a number of
aids and aſſiſtants to forward and
promote the ſervice).

Livres 300,726

Brought over Livres   301,526

TO WIT.

Salaries.

A Director General at .	6,000
A Sub-Director . . .	3,000
An Engineer	4,000
Two aids to do. the one at 2,400, and the other 1,600 livres	4,000
A Comptroller . . .	2,000
Two Warehousemen, one at 1,500, and the other at 1000 livres	2,500
A head Clerk and book-keeper	1,800
Two under Clerks, at 1,500 the one, and 1,000 livres the other	2,500
A Surgeon	2,000
An Apothecary . . .	1,500
A Chaplain	1,200
A Steward of the Infirmary	600

Livres   31,100

Livres   301,526

O   A

Brought over Livres   301,526

Salaries brought over   31,100

A Mafter Baker . . .   720

A journeyman to do. .   500

A Superintendant of the
Teams, &c. 1,200

An aid to do.   500

Two Supervifors for Ship-
ping and landing the
cargoes 1,440

The Mafter General of the
Forges 3,000

A Superintendant of the
Coal Works . . . 2,000

A Mafter Carpenter to lot
out the feveral forts of
wood 2,400

A Mafter Blackfmith . . 1,200

Three affiftants at 400 livres
each 1,200

A Mafter Mafon 1,200

Livres   46,460

Livres   301,526

Six

Brought over Livres   301,526
Salaries brought over   46,460

Six journeymen to do. at
   400 livres each . . .   2,400
A Master Joiner . . .   1,000
Two journeymen to do.
   the one at 500, and the
   other 600 livres . . .   1,100
A Master Wheel-Wright   1,000
Two journeymen to do.
   the one at 500, and the
   other at 600 livres . .   1,100
A Harness Maker, or Sadler   720
A journeyman to do. . .   500
A Head Gardener . .   1,000
Two under Gardeners, the
   one at 400 livres, the other
   at 500 livres   900
Six Day Labourers, at 400
   livres each   2,400
Total amount of the
   Salaries . . . Livres 58,580   58,580

     Livres   360,106

O 2   *Art.*

Brought over *Livres*   360,106

Art. XIV. The unforeseen Ex-
pences.

In fine, to make a sufficient allowance for contingencies, or unforeseen expences, such as journies,
office charges, postage of letters,
purchase of books, instruments,
the making of chymical experiments, the premiums given for
encouragement : these different
articles are rated at the collec-
tive of   9,894

Total Livres 370,000

We have entered into a minute detail of
the annual disbursements in the proposed
enterprise, and we find they amount to
370,000 livres. In this estimate, is comprised
the sum of 6,000 livres for the commercial
interest of the capital sunk, in the extraordinary advances made at the commencement
of the establishment. It remains now to
eftimate

eftimate the produce of this operation, in order to afcertain the profits arifing therefrom.

Art. XV. The Produce.

The three principal articles of produce, the quantity and price of which, fuppofing them delivered at Marfeilles, have been fully detailed above, and are as follow :

1ft. Timber and Planks.

2d. Wood for fuel.

3d. Iron in it's raw ftate, with a due allowance for the quantity of native fteel, which confiderably enhances the value of a great part of the iron.

Forty thoufand feet of timber or planks, which may be obtained from 2000 cords, fet apart for that ufe, at 40 fols per cubic foot delivered at Marfeilles or any other port in the Mediterrean will produce 80,000

O 3   Six

Brought over Livres . 80,000

Six thoufand weight of fire wood
form 600 cords, at three livres
per weight 180,000

Twenty thoufand quintals of forged
iron at 18 livres per quintal a-
voirdupois, makes, in the whole,
the fum of 360,000

Total Livres 620,000

Art. XVI. The Balance.

The annual expence comprifing
the neceffary fum for the re-
inburfing the primary capital
for the extraordinary advances
makes 370,000

The annual produce amounts to . 620,000

Balance in favour of the annual pro-
fits, accruing to the Company,
Livres 250,000

Art,

Art. XVII. Sundry advantages accruing to the State.

From the above fum of annual profits (250,000) we have only to make a reduction, in reality a confiderable one, but which has for object an article that the author had principally in view, when he drew up this MEMORIAL, viz. the direct and immediate advantages accruing to the ftate, or the department of Corfica in particular, from this, or fimilar undertakings, that may be formed in this ifland.

It is the intereft of every government that individuals fhould enrich themfelves by induftry, and by employing their refpective capitals in the cultivation of profitable arts. But as a revenue is requifite for the maintenance of a force fufficient to preferve good order, individuals fhould contribute to the formation of this revenue, by a voluntary facrifice, on their part, of an equal fhare of their profits. The medium of direct im-

O 4   pofts

pofts being in the kingdom the four twentieths, or the one fifth of the general revenue,
the company, whofe operations have been
detailed above, and whofe annual profits refulting from the exertion of it's induftry,
and the advances of a very confiderable capital, would amount to two hundred and
fifty thoufand livres, fhould contribute to
the Provincial Exchequer about fifty thoufand, or the fifth part of its profits. Agreeable to this plan it is propofed to lay a pro-
portional duty on the various produce
arifing to the company from the privilege of
exploiting the forefts in the ifland of Corfica,

Art. XVIII. Duties impofed on the exports of
Wood and Iron.

The exploitation of the domain of GALE-
RIA, divided into forty years, would yield
an annual produce to the amount of fixteen
thoufand cords. Suppofing that the faid quantity of wood was divided into three diftinct
parts, and their refpective ufes afcertained as
follows ; viz. the amount of two thoufand
cords

cords for timber and planks, which would yield forty thoufand cubic feet: fix thou- fand cords for firewood, and eight thoufand cords to be converted into charcoal, with which twenty thoufand quintals of iron might be forged,

Therefore it is propofed to impofe a duty of five fols per cubic foot on timber in general exported from Corfica, which, for forty thou- fand cubic feet would produce the fum of 10,000

Twenty fols per cord for fire wood exported, would yield for fix thoufand cords 6,000

Thirty fols per quintal, of forged iron, would produce for 20,000 quintals. 30,000

Total Livres   46,000

This fum amounts nearly to the fifth part of the profits above fpecified ; and if it

is

is confidered, that the part of the wood capable of yielding fuch a revenue is the one fortieth part of the woods in Corfica, it will appear, that this ifland, which actually does, and moreover has for thefe twenty years paft, coft the ftate the annual fum of nine hundred thoufand livres, can be able to fupply its own exigencies; as its annual income would amount to one million, eight hundred, and forty thoufand livres. Befides, this revenue being no more than one fifth part of the profits of other companies that might enter upon fuch an undertaking, would occafion in the province a circulation of an encreafed capital of triple, or quadruple value.

*Art. XIX. The particular advantages accru-
ing to the Province.*

- The advantages of eftablifhments of this nature, if fet on foot, and feconded by due encouragement, throughout Corfica, would be very great and extenfive.

ROADS

ROADS, which are as it were the rich veins
of a commercial and well regulated country,
would, by means of thefe improvements,
be multiplied in every direction, as well as
the *bridges.*

The WOODS and moſt deſerted ſpots
would be peopled with inhabitants by degrees, and become more and more accef-
ſible and connected.

The WATERS ſtopped in their courſes,
and formed into reſervoirs, would fill the
canals deſtined to enable the pipes to act at
the forges, in lieu of bellows ; they might
likewiſe ſerve to irrigate the neighbouring
grounds ; and a country which receives,
from rain and melted ſnows, one half more
water than all France put together, would no
longer ſuffer from an abſolute want of
watering which is occaſioned by the rapid
declivity of its lands, that carry off the
waters from the mountains into the ſea,
without the inhabitants deriving the leaſt
benefit from ſo manifeſt an advantage.

Lands

[204]

Lands hitherto neglected would improve from culture, and amply repay, by a grateful return, the induſtrious farmer for his pains. By giving thus a fuitable direction to the waters, they would facilitate the formation of artificial meadows, a thing totally unknown in Corſica : yet cultivators in general conſider this ſyſtem as the very eſſence of rural economy.

The free circulation of air would be eſtabliſhed in the *Gorges* (the narrow paſſes and defiles of mountains) and this very air would be purified by the continual fires there would be over the ſeveral parts of the iſland. This is a circumſtance truly important, and well worth being attended to, as the country is known to be very unhealthy.

If due attention was paid to the fabricating and manufacturing of iron, induſtry would, in its various branches, aſſume freſh vigour, and call forth the aid of many fecondary arts. This would provide uſeful occupation to numbers.

A

A feafonable encouragement to induftry would highly favour population, and augment the natural refources of the ifland by giving vent to the fale of the productions of the country.

Foreign companies, which alone are capable of fetting on foot an eftablifhment of this nature on a large and extenfive fcale, would caufe a great circulation of fpecie over the different parts of the ifland ; a part of this fpecie might be laid out in the purchafing woods from thofe communities, or individuals, who are of themfelves incapable of turning them to any advantage. This arrangement would tend to enrich the one and the other by ways and means, of which they had neither of them entertained the leaft notion.

In a word, an extenfive fabrication of iron, in Corfica, once eftablifhed, it would be an eafy matter to erect a number of workfhops for carrying on the feveral branches of this important bufinefs; from the firft

ftate

ftate, which is in *pigs* and *bars*, the iron
has to pafs progreffively through the different degrees of refinement, till it obtains
from the fkilful artificer, a final polifh ; af-
fecting then the brilliancy of the diamond,
this metal difdains its original name, and
is converted into what is called fteel.
This is the ne plus ultra of mechanic perfection and ingenuity. Wood and water
are the two effentials in the working of
iron.

The finding occupation for the forefts in
Corfica would prove a feafonable relief to
the fouth of France, where they experience
at the prefent moment a great dearth of
wood, owing to the vaft confumption
which has been made of this valuable commodity of late years.

CON-

CONCLUSION AND PETITION.

THE UNDERWRITTEN PETITIONER presumes to set forth, THAT, actuated by a concern and zeal for the Public Weal, as well as his own private interest, during a residence of four years in the island of Corsica, has carefully enquired into and ascertained the means of forming the most useful establishments in the country. In spite of every natural obstacle, he finds, after the most minute investigation of the subject, THAT, the Woods in this Province form a most important and inestimable object of INDUSTRY, and constitute an intrinsic and permanent RESOURCE. The UNDERWRITTEN furthermore submits it as his opinion, THAT the EXPLOITATION of the Forests, the establishing iron forges and manufactories would prove the infallible means of regenerating CORSICA.

Convinced of the certainty of success in this, or a similar establishment, the PETI-

2 TIONER

TIONER wifhes, on a liberal and extenfive plan, to undertake the faid enterprife, at the fole *expence* and *rifk* of SELF AND COMPANY. By adopting this fyftem of Adminiftration, Government will be fhortly enabled to raife a REVENUE in this Province fufficient to DEFRAY THE EXPENCES it occafions.

The PETITIONER, therefore, PROPOSES, by way of trial, to *exploit* all the greater and leffer woods *(Forefts* and *Makis)* in the DOMAIN OF GALERIA, according to the plan here laid down. The faid Domain appertains to the Crown, and is fituated on the Weftern Coaft of the Ifland. HE ENTREATS the NATIONAL ASSEMBLY to take the *premifes* into their moft ferious *confideration,* and he *(the Petitioner)* humbly hopes, and moft refpectfully folicits a grant, or exclufive privilege, for the term of forty years enfuing, of that extenfive CONCHA, (Beach) which is formed by the numerous torrents that difcharge themfelves into the fea, near the Tower and Port of Galeria.

The

The UNDERWRITTEN, offers to pay five sols duty per cubic foot for all the timber hewn, or sawed, that he shall export from the island ; twenty sols for all firewood per cord ; and thirty sols per quintal for all forged or fabricated iron : and he REPEATS, That in confideration of the faid grant for exploitation made in his favour, or for his perfonal ufe and benefit, he WILL PAY to the State an annual fum of forty to fifty thoufand livres for woods, which have hitherto been of no ufe to the Public, for want of the neceffary roads, and which never can become profitable, but by employing a very confiderable capital, duly adminiftered and feconded by every effort of induftry.

One fifth of the above mentioned duties, the PETITIONER PROPOSES to allow to the PIEVE DE NIOLO, declaring at the fame time that he is ready and willing on his part to remove every oppofition refpecting the *claim* which the INHABITANTS of the faid parifh lay to certain woods within the jurifdiction of Galeria. Now, as the matter

P   in

in litigation is merely contefted for the fake
of the pafture grounds, other lands of equal
fertility might be ceded to the Pieve upon a
much better title. This arrangement might
be eafily effected, as there is a plenty of pafture land within the Domain. This will
conciliate the common intereft of the Pieve,
the Department, and the State, at one and
the fame time.

AND, FINALLY, the PETITIONER entreats the NATIONAL ASSEMBLY, in
confideration of his great zeal and attention,
not to permit him to fuftain the heavy lofs
of his paft labours, through the frivolous
objections of thofe who are themfelves incapable of propofing a better fcheme, which
is founded on the very nature of the objects
in view, and calculated to regenerate the
Ifland of Corfica. The producing a NEW
REVENUE of fifteen hundred thoufand livres
fufficient to anfwer every exigency whatever of the adminiftration of the Province:
The faving to the Public Treafury the fum
of nine hundred thoufand livres, hitherto

fet

fet apart for this purpofe; an expence that muft neceffarily be continued, at leaft in part, if this plan be rejected upon weak and trivial confiderations : In a word, an increafe of induftry in favor of Corfica, to the amount of more than twenty millions per annum, are motives fufficiently cogent to induce the UNDERWRITTEN to hope, that he will not be deprived of the permiffion of proving, to demonftration, the goodnefs and folidity of this his plan. The experiments will be made at his own expence, on a fixed Canton, or lot of wood, which is of no confiderable advantage to any body.

In RETURN, it is more than probable, that he will be enabled to pay unto the State, in the fpace of forty years, a fum not lefs than fixteen or eighteen hundred thou-fand livres.

FOCARD DE CHATEAU.

ERRATA.

The Reader will perceive that the sum carried over to p. 189, is 800 *livres* less than the total of p. 188. The first and last lines of that and the three following pages are, in consequence, incorrect. The error has been rectified in the succeeding pages.

CONTENTS to the APPENDIX.

viii   CONTENTS.

www.ingramcontent.com/pod-product-compliance
Lightning Source LLC
Chambersburg PA
CBHW030326270326
41926CB00010B/1515